"Sharon Besser and Ruslana Westerlund's *Making Language Visible in Social Studies* is a must-read resource for anyone who is passionate about teaching for equity through social studies. Their practical, empowering, and language-based disciplinary literacy approach provide teachers with a unique and effective path to maximally improve their students' disciplinary expertise in social studies."

Dr. Andrés Ramírez, *Associate Professor in the Department of Curriculum and Instruction at Florida Atlantic University*

"*Making Language Visible in Social Studies* offers teachers of social studies the essential 'behind the scenes' support to integrate attention to the language and content of social science. The authors address both the 'what' of key disciplinary texts for learning and the 'how' of pedagogic practice, including authentic texts and practical activities to engage and support literacy for learning in social science."

Sally Humphrey, *Senior Lecturer, School of Education, Australian Catholic University*

"This book is a much-needed collection for teachers and teacher educators in need of resources to develop their knowledge base about how language is used in social studies. With practical concepts, ideas, and tools, this book will empower teachers to teach language in the context of social studies disciplinary genres. Chapters illustrate problems of practice with annotated social studies texts showing language features and functions that can be used in curriculum design and practical applications for both content and language teachers."

Luciana C. de Oliveira, *Ph.D., Professor and Associate Dean for Academic Affairs and Graduate Studies, School of Education, Virginia Commonwealth University*

"Social Studies teachers are literacy teachers. This book clearly shows what these teachers need to know about language and how to teach it in the context of social studies classes for the benefit of students' acquisition of knowledge and ability to function as literate individuals."

María Estela Brisk, *Boston College, Emeritus Professor*

Making Language Visible in Social Studies

As the first book in the Making Disciplinary Language Visible series, this practical toolkit helps teachers promote disciplinary literacy development for Multilingual learners and their peers in the 5–12 social studies classroom. Using systemic functional linguistics (SFL) and the SFL-informed genre pedagogy, the Teaching and Learning Cycle for Disciplinary Genres, the book shows teachers how to teach content using language as a meaning-making resource. Besser and Westerlund provide clear guidance on understanding how language is used in the discipline and provide practical tools to empower teachers to teach language in the service of social studies disciplinary genres.

Chapters feature authentic vignettes to illustrate problems of practice, annotated social studies texts, practical curriculum design tools, exercises for readers to develop knowledge about language, and sample scripts for practical application.

Sharon Besser is a teacher educator, curriculum writer, and researcher who looks at problems in education through the lens of Systemic Functional Linguistics. She has over 25 years of experience locally and internationally in support of Multilingual learners.

Ruslana A. Westerlund is an educational consultant, author, keynote speaker, and researcher of disciplinary literacy through Systemic Functional Linguistics with more than 25 years of experience in the field of Multilingual learner education.

Making Disciplinary Language Visible
Sharon Besser, Series Editor
Ruslana A. Westerlund, Series Editor

Making Language Visible in Social Studies: A Guide to Disciplinary Literacy in the Social Studies Classroom
Sharon Besser and Ruslana A. Westerlund

Making Language Visible in Social Studies

A Guide to Disciplinary Literacy in the Social Studies Classroom

Sharon Besser and
Ruslana A. Westerlund

NEW YORK AND LONDON

Designed cover image: © Getty Images

First published 2024
by Routledge
605 Third Avenue, New York, NY 10158

and by Routledge
4 Park Square, Milton Park, Abingdon, Oxon, OX14 4RN

Routledge is an imprint of the Taylor & Francis Group, an informa business

© 2024 Taylor & Francis

The right of Sharon Besser and Ruslana A. Westerlund to be identified as authors of this work has been asserted in accordance with sections 77 and 78 of the Copyright, Designs and Patents Act 1988.

All rights reserved. No part of this book may be reprinted or reproduced or utilised in any form or by any electronic, mechanical, or other means, now known or hereafter invented, including photocopying and recording, or in any information storage or retrieval system, without permission in writing from the publishers.

Trademark notice: Product or corporate names may be trademarks or registered trademarks, and are used only for identification and explanation without intent to infringe.

ISBN: 978-1-032-29919-8 (hbk)
ISBN: 978-1-032-28822-2 (pbk)
ISBN: 978-1-003-30271-1 (ebk)

DOI: 10.4324/9781003302711

Typeset in Optima
by KnowledgeWorks Global Ltd.

Sharon dedicates this book to the Berkeley Broads, you inspire me to make this a better world.

Ruslana dedicates this book to all the Ukrainian students who continue going to school in the time of war and whose resilience and fierce faith in the future and victorious Ukraine inspires us all.

Contents

Meet the Authors   x
Acknowledgments   xi

1. **What Does It Mean to Make Language Visible in Social Studies and Why Do We Need to Do It?**   1
2. **What Is the Nature of Language in Social Studies Explanations? What Do We Mean by Explain?**   24
3. **What Is the Nature of Language of Arguments in Social Studies? What Do We Mean by Argue?**   60
4. **How to Make Language Visible Using the Teaching and Learning Cycle for Disciplinary Genres**   93
5. **A Language-Based Approach to Disciplinary Reading**   141

Meet the Authors

Sharon Besser, Ph.D., is a teacher educator, researcher, and curriculum writer. She received her doctorate from U.C. Berkeley in language and literacy education. Ruslana Westerlund, Ed.D., is a Ukrainian-born writer, researcher, and educational consultant. She received her doctorate from Bethel University. Sharon and Ruslana met at a Systemic Functional Linguistics (SFL) affinity group in Madison, Wisconsin, while Sharon was working at Edgewood College teaching teachers about language and Ruslana was working at WIDA as an associate researcher. Since meeting, they have done several classroom-based research projects together, led countless workshops for teachers, and created numerous publications together. They specialize in using SFL to make equity visible in every classroom, not just on websites in school districts' mission statements. Their approach for making equity visible is done through explicit teaching of disciplinary genres for all students through scaffolding up and not simplifying down, which is the foundation of the humanizing pedagogy of promise. They are driven by the vision to transform schools where all teachers are equipped with the right knowledge about language that empowers them to use language as a vehicle for learning and engaging with life itself, not as an inventory of structures. Their unique area of expertise and research is writing in the disciplines through an apprenticeship pedagogy called the Teaching and Learning Cycle for Disciplinary Genres (TLC-DG). When they are not talking about language in education, they discuss sourdough bread making and kombucha brewing. This is their first book together.

Acknowledgments

We are profoundly grateful to the many people who have inspired and supported our work. We are particularly indebted to the teachers we have worked with over the years who have invited us into their classrooms, around their dinner tables, and have participated with us in countless opportunities of learning and collaboration.

We are deeply appreciative of our mentors, who have contributed significantly to our understanding of language learning and SFL. Specifically, Sharon would like to thank Lily Wong Fillmore for setting her on the path of finding ways to draw attention to language for teachers and Jed Hopkins, whose creative and playful approach to genre pedagogy brings joy to our field. Ruslana would like to thank Mariana Castro, who assigned her a task of researching the language of development of the early years. That search led her to discover Halliday's work of analyzing his son's language from functional perspective and later Claire Painter's work. She is also indebted to her mentor, Sally Humphrey, and her patient explanations of the SFL metafunctions in a coffee shop in Sydney in 2016. She is also profoundly thankful to Luciana de Oliveira, whose article Nouns in History changed the way she see "vocab" in social studies texts.

Lastly, we would like to thank our colleagues, friends, and family who read drafts and provided valuable feedback and support, particularly Rob Westerlund, Sean and Adelaide Howell, and Lydia Wegert.

Graphic Design by Dmytro Komarynski.

What Does It Mean to Make Language Visible in Social Studies and Why Do We Need to Do It?

YOUNG PEOPLE need strong tools for, and methods of, clear and disciplined thinking in order to traverse successfully the worlds of college, career, and civic life.

(C3 Framework, p. 15)

The Common Core State Standards for English Language Arts and Literacy in History/Social Studies, Science, and the Technical Subjects call on social studies teachers to share in the responsibilities for literacy instruction in K-12 education.

(NGA and CCSSO, 2010a as cited in C3 Framework, p. 20)

"What does liberty look like?" This is a compelling question from one of the inquiries from the College, Career, and Civics (C3) Framework for Social Studies, designed to be used in History, Civics, Geography, or Economics. We are going to use this cartoon (Figure 1.1) to illustrate what it means to make language visible in social studies and why we need to do it. Hopefully, the cartoon gave you a little chuckle, and if so, why? What's funny about Lina's (student on the right) response, "Liberty is a green lady with a torch." Would there be a context in which this would be the preferred response? The Statue of Liberty is indeed a tall green lady with a torch. Likewise, Marcus's (student on the left) argument that economic prosperity is a hallmark of liberty can also be made in response to the prompt. However, as you no doubt know, Marcus's response is appropriate for the context, and Lina's is not. How do we know this?

DOI: 10.4324/9781003302711-1

Making Language Visible in Social Studies

Figure 1.1 Cartoon with a teacher drawing on the board
Credit: Adelaide Howell

Let's unpack the context. First, it's a high school economics class. High school economics classes have predictable content having to do with income, trade, cash, and spending. So a response to "What does liberty look like?" in the context of an economics class is going to include this kind of content. Second, the assignment is to write a five-paragraph essay. This implies a structure that includes an introduction, three body paragraphs, and a conclusion. If the teacher had left it at that, we couldn't be sure what kind of essay. Is it supposed to be a literary response, explanation, and argument? A literary response doesn't make sense in the context of an economics class, but both explanations and arguments do. Fortunately, the teacher said, "And don't forget Claim, Evidence, Reasoning." This narrows the type of essay to an argument. The context, therefore, comes with a set of parameters, expectations, and even rules that need to be understood and followed. Lina did not follow the parameters, either because she didn't know them or chose to ignore them. Marcus seemed to know these expectations and followed them.

We can say that Marcus is developing an awareness of *disciplinary literacy* in the context of 11th Grade Economics. Let's start with a discussion on what we mean by disciplinary literacy.

What Is Disciplinary Literacy?

The view of disciplinary literacy we take up in this book is multidimensional. It is the specific way of knowing, reasoning, reading, writing, doing, believing, and communicating by members of a particular discipline. Disciplinary literacy encompasses three central aspects of disciplinary learning: Discourses and practices, identities, and knowledge (Moje, 2008). Disciplinary literacy is concerned with pursuing habits of mind valued by the community. Disciplines represent "cultures, ... [with] their own conventions and norms that are highly specialized to particular purposes and audiences" (Moje, 2015, p. 273). Part of learning in a subject area, then, is coming to understand the "norms of practice" for constructing and communicating disciplinary knowledge (Lemke, 1990; Moje, 2007; Wineburg & Martin, 2004). Part of that learning also involves examining how disciplinary norms for practice are similar to or different from the everyday norms for practice. Such learning requires understanding deeply held assumptions or themes of the discipline (Lemke, 1990).

One important dimension of disciplinary literacy we will focus on in this book is an understanding that language exists to serve the content. Language exists in the service of learning. When we make the language patterns visible, we do a better job at expressing and understanding the content. When we do that, we and our students get better at the content. Disciplinary literacy is all about figuring out how language realizes the content of the discipline and teaching into that so our students get that too. In short, this is an approach that pays attention to the unique ways members of each disciplinary community read, write, reason, value, think, communicate, and create (see, e.g., Achugar et al., 2007; Fang, 2020; Fang & Schleppegrell, 2010). Disciplinary communities can be conceived of in many forms, such as book clubs, podcast audiences, organic farmers, sourdough bakers, historians, and 11th Grade Economics classes, to name a few. Each of these communities has what we call *disciplinary literacy practices*, processes of going about making meaning that the community creates that represent their unique way of reading, writing, reasoning, valuing, thinking, communicating, and creating. These disciplinary literacy practices can change, evolve, and push boundaries, as the practices exist to serve the meaning the community is putting out into the world. Practices may include developing arguing from evidence, pursuing inquiries, asking compelling questions, identifying and challenging perspectives, constructing explanations and arguments, and others. Each community has expectations and parameters that best work to make the meaning that serves the goals of the community. Schools are typically organized into disciplinary communities: English, Science, Social Studies, Math with those communities being divided into smaller communities: World Literature, Biology, Civics, Algebra 11. As you read this book, you'll note many references to the College, Career, and Civic Life (C3) Framework for State Social Studies Standards (2013), the C3 Framework for short. This is one of the disciplinary communities we authors, and this book, are a part of. One of the main jobs of a learner in those communities is to figure out the expectations and parameters. It's like figuring out what the teacher wants in the context of the disciplinary community. Let's take a look at Figure 1.2.

Now, consider this. Many disciplinary communities share disciplinary literacy practices. For example, five-paragraph essays, narrative descriptions, explanations, lab reports, and informational reports are common ways that the learning is displayed in many disciplinary

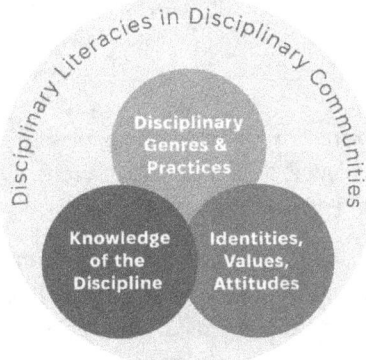

Figure 1.2 Multidimensional view of disciplinary literacy

communities in middle and high school. However, these practices look different depending on the community. Arguments are a good example of this. The way scientists engage in argumentation is different from the way scholars of literature craft literary response arguments in English Language Arts (ELA) with one similarity being that they both require evidence to support one's claims. While scientists draw their evidence from data in experiments and observations, evidence in ELA comes from texts, for example, images and ideas that support a theme, as in theme interpretation essays. In social studies, particularly within the C3 Framework, learners follow the C3 Inquiry Arc: Develop compelling questions, weigh evidence, and construct explanations and arguments. Providing evidence is a different process in each discipline, but how, what makes it different?

What makes it different is *how* the discipline communities use language in service of the content. In this way, language is a resource for serving the goals of the disciplinary processes and concepts (Derewianka & Jones, 2023; Martin & Rose, 2007; Schleppegrell, 2004). Another way to say this is that the difference between an argument in ELA and one in social studies is not just the content, but *how language resources are used to create disciplinary meanings.*

Let's shift our focus to social studies. Typically, content is expressed through arguments and explanations which have predictable patterns unique to social studies (Coffin, 2009; Schleppegrell, 2004). The authors of the Common Core State Standards (CCSS) and the C3 Framework framed the standards around the expectations for students to engage in processes and make meaning in social studies specific ways. Take a look at these standards from the C3 Framework, Dimension 4, Communicating Conclusions:

> D4.1.9-12. Construct **arguments** using precise and knowledgeable claims, with evidence from multiple sources, while acknowledging counterclaims and evidentiary weaknesses.
>
> D4.2.9-12. Construct **explanations** using sound reasoning, correct sequence (linear or nonlinear), examples, and details with significant and pertinent information and data, while acknowledging the strengths and weaknesses of the explanation given its purpose (e.g., cause and effect, chronological, procedural, technical).
>
> D4.3.9-12. Present adaptations of **arguments and explanations** that feature evocative ideas and perspectives on issues and topics to reach a range of audiences and venues outside the classroom *using print and oral technologies (e.g., posters, essays, letters, debates, speeches, reports, and maps) and digital technologies (e.g., Internet, social media, and digital documentary).*
>
> (C3 Framework, p. 60)
>
> Key:
>
> - **Disciplinary literacy practices: Construct arguments and explanations**
> - Social studies specific ways of thinking, reasoning, and connecting ideas
> - *Formats specific ways of communicating to an audience*

In the standards above, the disciplinary literacy practices (shown in bold) are named: Arguments and explanations. Types of social studies explanations (shown in regular text) are also named: Cause and effect, chronological, procedural, and technical. The social studies specific ways of thinking, reasoning, and connecting ideas (shown in italics) are named, for example, using precise and knowledgeable claims, acknowledging strengths and weaknesses of the explanation, evocative ideas and perspectives on issues and topics. Social studies specific ways of communicating are also named, for example, debates, speeches, and maps.

Additionally, from these standards, we can derive a structure for each of the disciplinary literacy practices. In D4.1.9-12., for example, the argument could be structured in the following way: Claim, Evidence 1, Evidence 2, Evidence 3, Counterclaim, Conclusion.

Why Do We Have an Equity Problem in Social Studies?

Let's go back to our cartoon for a moment. What if, instead of assigning a "five-paragraph Essay" on "What does liberty look like?," Ms. Williams had told the students she wanted an argument "using precise and knowledgeable claims, with evidence from multiple sources, while acknowledging counterclaims and evidentiary weaknesses" and "featuring evocative ideas and perspectives on issues and topics" to be presented in a digital documentary. Would that guidance have supported Lina in writing a piece that fits better into the disciplinary community of this high school economics class? What if Ms. Williams also included a suggested outline: Claim, Evidence 1, Evidence 2, Evidence 3, Counterclaim, Conclusion?

Being explicit about which disciplinary literacy practice, the purpose, the content and structure like this would, no doubt, support Lina's writing development, but it may not be enough. This would make Ms. Williams expectations and the expectations of the purpose of the piece more visible. However, what is still invisible is how you use language to write a claim, a counterclaim, etc.

Our research and teaching, and likely your own experience in working with students, have shown us that there is a large disparity among students in what they can and do produce. We have seen a big gap between students like Marcus who seems to produce essays that match the expectations of the discipline seemingly magically, just by being in the class. We know them as our "A" students. We have seen other students who can do proficient work with a little support related to the purpose and structure of the assignment, as suggested in the previous paragraph. These are our "B" students. And, we have seen many, and maybe even *most, students* miss the mark. Why? When we have a disparity in academic achievement, and we suspect this disparity is related to factors outside of the individual student, our field refers to this as an equity problem. What are these factors that contribute to a lack of equity? Here are a few relevant to this book:

- White privilege as it relates to early literacy experiences. This refers to the 100s, if not 1000s, of hours that some (often White middle and upper class) parents spend reading with their children before they get to school, which gives these children a huge advantage in learning to read once they get to school.
- Systemic racism in education. This refers to systems in schools that create and maintain racial inequality for people of color. Some of the symptoms are as follows: a lack of teachers of color, discipline problems that result in students of color being sent out of class and not getting the chance to participate in the reading and writing lessons in elementary school, middle school, and high school; a lack of engagement in school, which then occurs repeatedly resulting in students not having the skills they need to do the work in High School which then results in them not having the confidence to participate.
- Ineffective approaches to literacy instruction. These refer to reading and writing programs that do not result in students mastering these skills.

What those factors have in common is that they all result in unequal types of support that students get in learning to read and write throughout their school careers. We are not implying that all students need the same type of support; for example, multilingual students who are still developing their English need a great deal of language-focused support from highly trained teachers. What we are suggesting is that each of those factors results in some students getting more or better support (e.g., students who get effective approaches to literacy instruction or help from parents) and some students getting no support (e.g., because they have been repeatedly kicked out of class and told they are dismissed as "not good enough" or "don't have enough English"). When we don't support all our students with intention, we are left with a great disparity in achievement within the class. So not providing support becomes an equity issue. Think about this for a minute in relation to your own teaching context:

- Whose job is it to teach middle and high school students how to write and read?

- Who among the students is participating in lessons that focus on writing and reading?
- Who is not participating?

Often, the job of teaching reading and writing falls to either elementary school teachers or ELA (English Language Arts) teachers. ESL (English as a Second Language) teachers have the job of teaching English language. In some middle and high schools, reading teachers teach remedial reading. The job of the social studies teacher is to teach content such as revolutions and human rights, shifting landforms, and governments, then and now. Each teacher typically works within their own department, and it is rare that teachers collaborate across them. From the student's perspective, then, there is no connection between reading, writing, language, and content.

This may have been acceptable prior to the CCSS and C3 Framework, but the expectations as framed in those standards and the curriculum in service of them are more rigorous than before. These standards are designed around mastery of social studies disciplinary literacy. In order to meet them, what is required is deep expertise and experience as a member of the social studies disciplinary community, with a great deal of mentoring and practice writing and reading in the unique way that is required for the discipline of social studies. This requires a shift in the work and expertise of us social studies teachers. Because we are expecting students to master the disciplinary practices specific to social studies, it is now imperative that this support takes place in the context of the discipline of social studies. By this we mean, in social studies classes by social studies teachers. Think about this for a moment:

- How can we promote equity and dismantle systemic racism as social studies teachers?
- What kind of support do students need in social studies to master disciplinary literacy?
- How can we provide this support to all students?
- How can we increase student participation and engagement?

We have been teachers and worked with teachers who are not exactly sure how to teach writing and reading in a way that would promote equitable access to the knowledge necessary to make meaning in the unique way that is valued in social studies. Making language visible in our disciplines takes knowledge about language and language patterns. This places new demands on teachers who are called to provide specific kinds of instructional support (Fang & Schleppegrell, 2010). Few teacher preparation programs address this, and most of us are more than a little squeamish about grammar, so we carry on teaching as we have been. This book is designed to do something different; it's going to teach you how to see language patterns in social studies texts, deepen your knowledge about language, and empower you to teach in a way that makes the language visible for your students. To do this, we will show you how to make language visible in your social studies community for the purpose of supporting all your students in mastering the ways of thinking, reading, writing, reasoning, and creating that serve the content you teach and the discipline more broadly.

Our Approach to Social Studies

Inquiry is at the heart of social studies teaching (Swan et al., 2018; C3 Framework and National Council for Social Studies[1]). As an instructional framework, inquiry-based teaching "builds out from the C3 Inquiry Arc through: (a) Compelling and supporting questions that frame and give structure to the inquiry (Dimension 1); (b) summative, formative, and additional performance tasks that provide the opportunities for communicating conclusions (Dimension 4); and (c) disciplinary sources that allow students to explore the compelling question, build content expertise, and develop the disciplinary skills to successfully support and defend their ideas (Dimensions 2 & 3)."

Both the C3 and the National Council for Social Studies emphasize that explanations and argumentation are not something that happen at the end of the unit but need to be integrated throughout. The inquiry approach takes place across the unit of instruction and involves supporting students in questioning and analysis, supporting students' thinking, reasoning, and reading, and providing explicit instruction in literacy practices.[2] In addition to the explicit and sustained instruction in disciplinary literacy practices, we want to add explicit and systematic teaching of language of social studies genre (Figure 1.3). The next section will define explicit and systematic instruction in the language of social studies genres from a functional perspective.

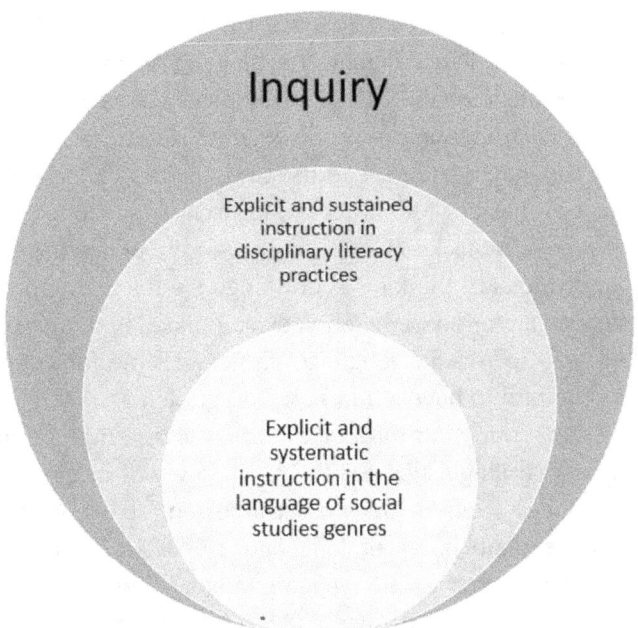

Figure 1.3 Pedagogical framework for making language visible

Our Approach to Teaching Language in Social Studies: What Is a Functional Perspective and How Will This Help Promote Equity?

Often when teachers think about teaching from a functional perspective, they think about functions such as arguing, explaining, presenting ideas. These are, of course, things we do with language, but as explained above, we need to go deeper into how we actually do these things. For example, how exactly do you "acknowledge a counterclaim" or "feature an evocative idea?" Expert social studies teachers like you know how to do this, probably without thinking too much. You have a toolbox full of language resources that give you lots of choices you pull from to do the writing you need to do. For example, as we are writing this, we are pausing to consider, should we have said, "let's start with an example" instead of just "for example?" We are wondering about the difference those choices make. "Let's start with an example" builds a relationship with you, the reader because "let's" connotes something we are going to do together. "For example" doesn't build the same relationship, but it is efficient at setting up an example. We create our social studies meaning through all the choices we make with language, choices that we pull from our toolbox of language resources. Marcus seemed to know what language resources to use and choices to make to produce what the teacher is looking for and Lina, either chose not to, or, more likely, did not have access to this knowledge and repertoire of language resources.

It is not hard to start thinking about language this way, and once you start to draw your attention to the choices you make all the time, you'll be well on your way to making language choices visible for your students. However, it is helpful to have a framework to guide us.

The theory that underlies this book, and gives us a useful framework is Systemic Functional Linguistics (SFL)[3]. This theory was originally designed by Michael Halliday (e.g., Halliday & Matthiessen, 2014), who wanted to understand and explain how our language use differs depending on the social purpose. He famously said, we learn language, we learn through language, and we learn about language. He has inspired many scholars to use this theory to do many things in education such as identifying characteristics of genres (disciplinary practices) we use for school (Martin & Rose, 2007; Schleppegrell, 2004); critically analyzing educational practices (e.g., Brisk, 2023; Gebhard, 2019); and teaching teachers about language in a way that is practical and empowering (Derewianka & Jones, 2023; Humphrey et al., 2023). We like SFL for its usefulness in describing the integration of content, language, and literacy for teachers (Gebhard, 2019; Schleppegrell et al., 2004). Perhaps most exciting and relevant to you are the pedagogical implications. In this book, we use an SFL-informed pedagogy of apprenticeship, called the Teaching and Learning Cycle to promote a way to scaffold instruction in a way that fosters equity by insisting that all students have access to the language resources they need to meet the demands of school.

The Teaching Learning Cycle of Disciplinary Genres (TLC-DG) in Figure 1.4 provides a framework that supports teachers in teaching students these language resources in the context of authentic texts students need to write and read. We will show you how to use this pedagogical model and give you many examples of how to use this in your classroom later in the book. First, though, we need to introduce you to a way of describing and talking about these language resources that we typically use to make meaning in social studies so that you will have the confidence to teach these to your students. The rest of the chapter will introduce you to some SFL metalanguage and

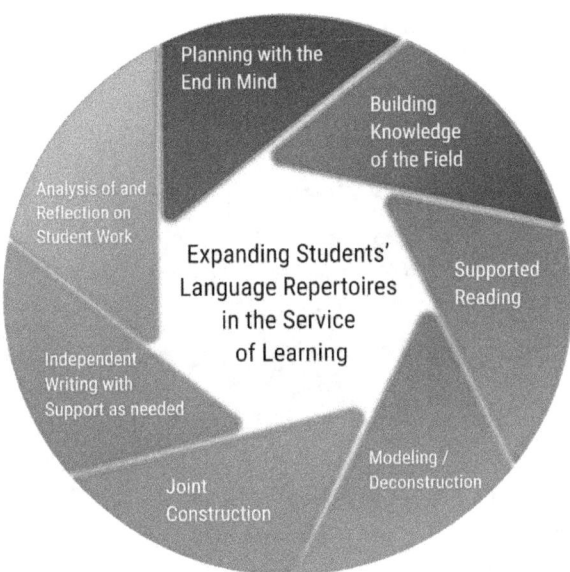

Figure 1.4 The teaching and learning cycle of disciplinary genres
Credit: Adapted from Derewianka and Jones (2023)

ways of thinking and describing language, all of which are foundational for the kind of teaching and learning you'll engage in throughout the book. Then, in the next two chapters, we build on this metalanguage and processes of drawing attention to language by focusing in detail on how we use language resources to craft explanations (Chapter 2) and arguments (Chapter 3).

This way of looking at language enables us to see how complex language is (Figure 1.5). Each circle has a component of language. They are nested in concentric circles to depict how choices in language are made simultaneously at the level of context, text, sentence, and word. Keep this in mind as you read this book. While there will be many times we will reference one ring of the circle at a time, we are always thinking about how the rings are interconnected.

Thinking about Texts at the Genre Level

Previously, when we talked about Ms. Williams changing the way she introduced her "What does liberty look like?" assignment to specifically explain that she wanted an argument "using precise and knowledgeable

Making Language Visible in Social Studies

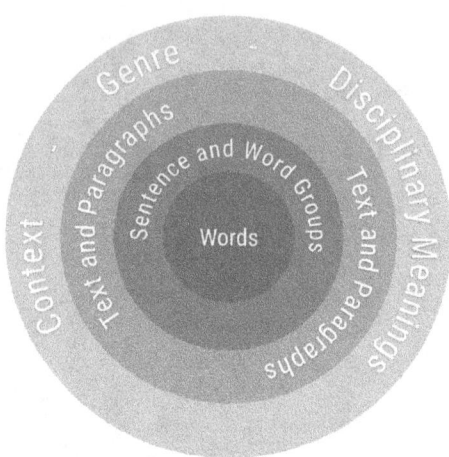

Figure 1.5 A stratified model of language
Credit: Adapted from Halliday and Matthiessen (2014)

claims, with evidence from multiple sources, while acknowledging counterclaims and evidentiary weaknesses," we were talking about the genre of the text. The term genre is widely and sometimes misleadingly used in education. We are using it very specifically here to pay attention to the social purpose of the whole text (including multimodal texts), the overall structure of the text that exists to meet that social purpose, and the specific job that each section of the text has in service of that purpose. Genres exist within and across disciplinary communities. In short, genre is about using language to achieve different purposes. This book focuses on the two main genres that we use most often in social studies to do the learning and teaching: Explanations and arguments.

Thinking about texts at the genre level requires us to think deeply about what kind of thinking and reasoning we want our students to do in service of the content. For example, do we want students to describe what something looks like, how one thing led to another, or the relationship between certain phenomena? All of these are legitimate ways of thinking in social studies, but as you saw in the cartoon, we need to be explicit with our students about which genre will best serve the content and reasoning around that content. In the next two chapters, we unpack explanations and then arguments, showing how to draw attention to the social purpose, generic structure that would serve that purpose, and how to identify the moves and jobs different sections of a piece of writing have. For example,

Making Language Visible in Social Studies

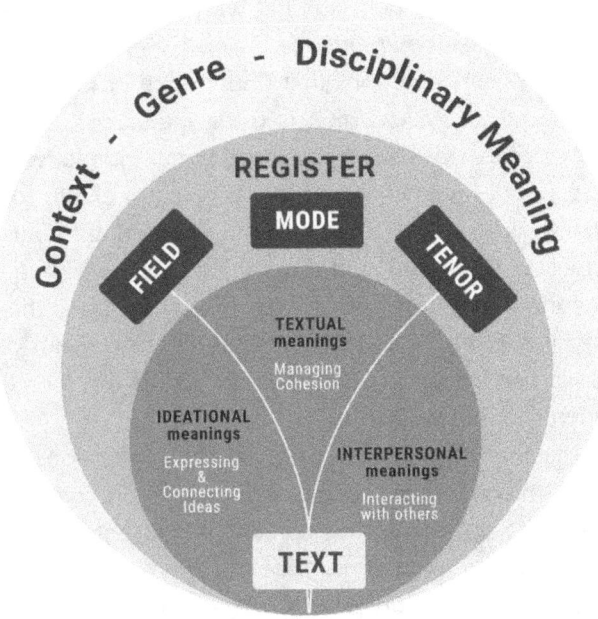

Figure 1.6 SFL trinocular view of register
Credit: Adapted from Derewianka and Jones (2023)

introductions don't just introduce, they orient the reader to the context, provide necessary background, and set up the reader to expect a certain type of reasoning (e.g., that this text will describe events that will have consequences or claims that will be supported in some way).

Thinking about social studies texts at the genre level makes visible the purpose, structure, and ways of reasoning, but we also need to think about *how* language enables us to achieve the purpose and illustrate our thinking and reasoning. To do that, we need to look at what SFL calls the register of the text (Figure 1.6).

Thinking about Texts at the Register Level

When we think about the register of the text, we describe the *how* of the text by making visible the language choices that express the content and meaning. We will group these language choices into three categories, each

15

that represents a different aspect of what we need to do in the texts. SFL refers to these aspects as *metafunctions*.

There are three metafunctions that underlie all of the ways we make meaning: Ideational, or *Field* which is using language to express ideas; interpersonal, or *Tenor* which is using language to interact with our audience; and textual, or *Mode* which is using language to create cohesive texts (e.g., Derewianka & Jones, 2023). As we make meaning in our disciplines and in any aspect of our social worlds, for that matter, we make use of each of these metafunctions simultaneously, most of the time without thinking about it. However, thinking about this in the context of our discipline is exactly what we need to do in order to make visible the specific ways we want our students to make meaning.

To guide our thinking, it's helpful to ask focus questions aligned with each metafunction. When we are thinking about Field, we ask, "How am I using language to get across my content? What types of grammatical features should I use to express my ideas?" When we are thinking about Tenor, we ask, "Who is my audience? Are they my peers or a distant adult audience? How formal or informal do I need to be? What kind of relationship do I want to build with my reader?" When we are thinking about Mode, we ask, "How should I lead my reader through the text? What sorts of ways can I weave the text together so it forms a cohesive whole?" This simultaneous interplay of these metafunctions comprises what we call the *register*. Differences between an email and a text, or an argument in social studies compared to one in ELA, or Marcus's text and Lina's text are essentially differences in the register of the texts. We will illustrate this below by returning to the student writing from our cartoon. You'll note we've added a few more lines in each of the texts.

As you study Table 1.1, notice the similarities and differences between Marcus and Lina's texts. We have organized this table by the metafunctions so you compare the texts and begin to notice how each author uses language to create meaning. Also note that we are looking at language descriptively here, as opposed to evaluatively, for the purpose of determining what choices the writers made.

This table is an example of a productive way of describing differences in writing pieces by focusing on language choices. Some of these choices are about what we typically think of as grammar, such as nouns and prepositions, and other choices don't fit as easily into grammatical categories, such as language to make a judgment. Let's look at the choices the

Table 1.1 Analysis of Student Work Using SFL Metafunctions

Metafunctions	Student texts	Focus questions
Field: Using language to express ideas and Using language to connect ideas	Liberty is a **tall green lady with a torch**. She is *in the New York Harbor*. This statue came *from France*....	How does Lina use language to get across the content? What types of grammatical features does she use to express her ideas? She describes the statue using a **long noun phrase** She describes where the statue is and how it got there using *prepositional phrases*
	<u>While some might argue differently</u>, my claim *is* that *liberty and prosperity go hand in hand*. First of all, you can't be free if you can't support yourself. Second of all …	How does Marcus use language to get across the content? What types of grammatical features does he use to express his ideas? He uses a *noun phrase* that connects the two main ideas He uses *is* to link the word claim to the actual claim He uses other *verbs* He previews a counterclaim by connecting <u>this clause</u> to his claim

(Continued)

Table 1.1 (Continued)

Metafunctions	Student texts	Focus questions
Tenor:		
Using language to interact with an audience	Liberty is a `tall green lady` with a torch. She is in the New York Harbor. This statue came from France....	Who is Lina's audience? How formal or informal is she being with this text? Her audience is Ms. Williams and she is using `informal language`
Using language to create interpersonal meaning		How neutral or judgmental is she being with this text? She is using a neutral tone, stating a series of facts
	While *some might argue differently*, my claim is that liberty and prosperity go <u>hand in hand</u>. First of all, <u>you can't be free</u> if you can't support yourself. Second of all ...	Who is Marcus's audience? How formal or informal is he being? His audience is Ms. Williams. He is mostly using a *formal tone*, although he uses <u>informal language too.</u> He also refers to the audience as "you" which creates solidarity with the reader
		How neutral or judgmental is he being with this text? He is being judgmental, using language that conveys his opinion, "liberty and prosperity go hand in hand"; "you can't be free if you can't support yourself"

(Continued)

Table 1.1 (Continued)

Metafunctions	Student texts	Focus questions
Mode: Using language to create cohesive texts	Liberty is a tall green lady with a torch. She is in the New York Harbor. This statue came from France....	How does Lina lead the reader through the text? Each sentence starts with the subject of the essay, liberty How is she making the text hang together as a whole? She uses a pronoun reference and a synonym for Liberty (this statue) to create cohesion
	While some might argue differently, my claim is that liberty and prosperity go hand in hand. **First of all,** you can't be free if you can't support yourself. **Second of all** ...	How does Marcus lead the reader through the text? He uses **text connectives** How does he make the text hang together as a whole? He begins with some then narrows it to you which he repeats Also, he uses a synonym for liberty (free) to create cohesion

writers made to *express and connect their ideas*, Field. For example, Lina used a long noun phrase to describe what liberty looks like, "a tall green lady with a torch" and prepositional phrases describing where liberty is, "in the New York harbor." These language choices serve to express Lina's literal meaning in response to the prompt. Marcus made choices that express his understanding of the metaphorical meaning of liberty as in "liberty and prosperity." Next let's look at how the writers created *interpersonal meaning*, Tenor. Marcus uses judgment-type language that expresses his strong opinion, for example, "you can't be free …," whereas Lina is very neutral in her opinion about the topic, simply stating facts, for example, "The statue came from France." Lastly, let's look at how the writers create cohesive texts. It's difficult to see this with these short excerpts, but we can get a sense of the differences. Marcus uses signposts such as "First of all," while Lina uses pronoun referencing and renaming to show that the sentences logically go together, "liberty" … "she" … "this statue".

We are also hoping you noticed that in the table we describe the language the students use relatively objectively. We have not said Marcus is more advanced than Lina but simply described how both were using language resources. We are not evaluating their writing, but describing their language use. Why would this distinction be important? There are several important reasons, and these are foundational to this book. First of all, to make language visible in the service of supporting students, we need to be able to see and describe the language students are using and the language we want students to be able to use. Second, we want to validate what students know about language and bring to their work. We recognize that all students have a toolbox of language resources that they bring to school each day. We also want to challenge the notion that the formal or academic language that characterizes Marcus's work is better or more advanced than Lina's. Throughout our day we use language for all different purposes and make different choices depending on the context and social purpose. Our goal is for students to understand what parameters and sets of choices are appropriate for the social purpose they find themselves in. *Our view of language development is that it is an increasing repertoire or range of language resources from which to make choices as well as an expansion of what we can do with language.*

How Will This Book Help Teachers?

This book is for Professional Learning Circles, coaches, teacher educators, teachers and people in teacher education programs who teach disciplinary literacy, teachers who teach ELLs, teachers who teach students who speak dialects of English, mainstream social studies teachers who are using C3 Framework or their state standards informed by the C3 Framework,[4] and any practitioner concerned with inequitable language and literacy outcomes in grades 5–12. This book is designed to support you in taking up the challenge of teaching social studies in a way that promotes equitable achievement of disciplinary literacy so that all of your students work toward mastering the standards set out for them. This book will enable you to predict what types of texts and varieties of language students will need to be able to comprehend and produce to be successful in your social studies classes. You'll develop knowledge about social studies specific language, which will build your confidence in being able to support your students' development. As you work through this book, we know you'll be thinking about how this all would apply to your teaching, so we provide plenty of ideas for classroom application.

Throughout this book, we ask you to apply theory to practice by thinking and working through tasks and short exercises. There are "answers," in the Answer Key at the end of the chapter. We put in "answers" in quotes to acknowledge that there may be more than one way to do these tasks. The numbers on the exercises correspond with numbers in the Answer Key.

Our outcomes for you:

- Predict what types of texts and varieties of language your students will need to be able to comprehend and produce
- Build a metalanguage that you can use with students to talk about language
- Develop ways to promote and support language development
- Assess language development in discipline-specific ways

Table 1.2 shows your road map for the book.

Table 1.2 Road Map of Our Book: What Social Studies Teachers Need to Know about Language

Knowledge of written genres of school How disciplinary meaning of social studies is realized through written genres: The Book	
WHAT we need to know about the patterns of language?	HOW to make the patterns visible?
Knowledge of language at genre level: How explanations are structured (Chapter 2) How arguments are structured (Chapter 3) **Knowledge of language at register level:** Language features salient to explanations (Chapter 2) Language features salient to arguments (Chapter 3)	**Making language visible at genre and register levels:** Teaching and Learning Cycle of Disciplinary Genres (Chapter 4) Language-based Approach to Disciplinary Reading (Chapter 5)

Notes

1. https://c3teachers.org/inquiry-design-model/
2. https://www.socialstudies.org/meeting-common-core-standards-english-language-arts-argument-writing
3. https://c3teachers.org/inquiry-design-model/
4. https://www.socialstudies.org/standards/c3

References

Achugar, M., Schleppegrell, M., & Oteiza, T. (2007). Engaging teachers in language analysis: A functional linguistic approach to reflective literacy. *English Teaching: Practice and Critique*, 6(2), 8–24.

Brisk, M. (2023). *Engaging students in academic literacies: SFL genre pedagogy for K-8 classrooms* (2nd ed.). Routledge.

Coffin, C. (2009). *Historical discourse: The language of time, cause and evaluation*. Bloomsbury.

Derewianka, B., & Jones, P. (2023). *Teaching language in context* (3rd ed.). Oxford University Press.

Fang, F. (2020). Toward a linguistically informed, responsive and embedded pedagogy in secondary literacy instruction. *Journal of World Languages, 6*(1–2), 70–91.

Fang, Z., & Schleppegrell, M. J. (2010). Disciplinary literacies across content areas: Supporting secondary reading through functional language analysis. *Journal of Adolescent & Adult Literacy, 53*(7), 587–597.

Gebhard, M. (2019). *Teaching and researching ELLs' Disciplinary Literacies. Systemic functional linguistics in the context of U.S. school reform.* Routledge.

Halliday, M. A. K., & Matthiessen, C. M. I. (2014). *An introduction to functional grammar* (4th ed.). Routledge.

Humphrey, S., Droga, L., & Feez, S. (2023). *Grammar and meaning* (3rd ed.). PETTA.

Lemke, J. (1990). *Talking science: Language, learning, and values.* Ablex.

Martin, J. & Rose, D. (2007). *Working with discourse: Meaning beyond the clause.* Bloomsbury.

Moje, E. B. (2007). Developing socially just subject-matter instruction: A review of the literature on disciplinary literacy teaching. *Review of Research in Education, 31,* 1–44. http://www.jstor.org/stable/20185100

Moje, E. B. (2008). Foregrounding the disciplines in secondary literacy teaching and learning: A call for change. *Journal of Adolescent & Adult Literacy, 52*(2), 96–107.

Moje, E. B. (2015). Doing and teaching disciplinary literacy with adolescent learners: A social and cultural enterprise. *Harvard Educational Review, 85*(2), 254–278.

Schleppegrell, M. (2004). *The language of schooling. A functional linguistics perspective.* Routledge.

Schleppegrell, M., Achugar, M., & Oteíza, T. (2004). The grammar of history: Enhancing content-based instruction through a functional focus on language. *TESOL Quarterly, 38*(1), 67–93.

Swan, K., Lee, J., & Grant, S. G. (2018). *Inquiry design model: Building inquiries in social studies.* National Council for the Social Studies & C3 Teachers.

Wineburg, S. S., & Martin, D. (2004). Reading and rewriting history. *Educational Leadership, 62*(1), 42–45.

2 What Is the Nature of Language in Social Studies Explanations?
What Do We Mean by Explain?

Vignette:

Figure 2.1 Mr. Rodriguez's whiteboard

T: Today I want you to plan out your essay. Here is an Outline. What's the first thing you need to think about?
S: Have a thesis.
T: That's right, what are some ideas?
S1: The Boarding Schools were bad for the kids.
T: Ok, tell me more, why were they bad?
S1: Because the kids forgot their language.

T: Ok, so you could say the Boarding Schools were bad because the kids lost their language. Does that work for a thesis?

Ss: Yes.

T: Ok, does anyone have any questions or are you ready to get to work on planning? No? Ok, your Exit Ticket is your Outline (Figure 2.1).

What Does It Look Like When We Don't Make Language Visible?

As you can imagine, this class is studying the consequences of westward expansion of the United States in the late eighteenth to mid-nineteenth century with a focus on the Native Americans.

The vignette was the introduction to the assignment. Let's assume that the writing instruction students had received was limited to crafting a thesis statement, and that Mr. Rodriguez expects that, by 11th grade, students are skilled in essay writing. Let's also assume that Mr. Rodriguez is an excellent teacher, knowledgeable about the content and able to engage and motivate his students. But writing instruction is not yet in his wheelhouse. So later, when the students turn in their essays, he wonders what he can do to help the third of his class that didn't produce the essays that would meet the CCSS or C3 Standards (National Council for the Social Studies Standards (n.d.)) he was required to teach to. These students had thesis statements, but they didn't explain the consequences of the Boarding School movement. As we discussed in the previous chapter, what Mr. Rodriguez needs to *do* is to teach his students how to write in ways that serve the content of his discipline. As we saw in Chapter 1, as social studies teachers, we need to be able to predict the kind of language students need to use to participate in our discipline and teach them that language.

We might describe that what Mr. Rodriguez did in the vignette above was to introduce an assignment in a way that hid the language demands of the assignment. We might say that while the content of the assignment was made really clear, the language of this assignment was invisible. How is it invisible? First, the specific genre was not identified explicitly, nor were there models of the genre provided so that students could see what the target text should look like. Second, while Mr. Rodriguez provided an outline, it had no specifics that would guide students to writing a social studies explanation. One could use that outline in any discipline where a five-paragraph essay is required. Lastly, and most troublesome, was that there is no particular focus on the language needed to express the content in the context of the assignment. Specifically, there were no learning targets that would indicate what language resources would best serve the content.

How do we get from this vignette to a language-focused way of teaching social studies in a way that makes the language students need visible? We start by attending to the genre. We need to be very clear about what genre we are asking our students to comprehend and produce. In social studies, the main genres are explanations and arguments (Coffin, 2009; de Oliveira & Obenchain, 2019; Schleppegrell, 2004). This chapter will focus on explanations, and Chapter 3 will focus on arguments.

Purpose

This chapter is going to help you figure out how to talk to your students about the language they need to do the work of explaining for the social studies you teach. In addition, it is going to show you how to help your students expand the meanings they make and ultimately expand their social studies linguistic repertoire.

Part 1: Genre: What Are the Different Kinds of Explanations That Are Important in Social Studies?

To discover what kinds of explanations exist in social studies, let's take a look at a few examples from the C3 Inquiry Hub of sample inquiry units.[1] They all require that students will construct an explanation:

- **What are the working conditions like for children in the banana industry?** Discuss the issue of child labor in the banana industry using evidence from sources to support ideas. (Formative Performance Task,

Grade 5, 5.7 Economics, Fifth Grade Banana Trade Inquiry: What is the Real Cost of Bananas?)[2]

- **How were people affected by the Dust Bowl?** Write a paragraph about how people were affected by the Dust Bowl. (Formative Performance Task, Grade 8, Era.7.2.USH.6 Eighth Grade U.S. History Inquiry, Was the Dust Bowl a Perfect Storm?)[3]

- **How did the Opium Wars create foreign influence in China and how did the Chinese react?** Write 2–3 sentences describing how the Opium Wars created foreign influences in China and the Chinese reactions. (Formative Performance Task, 10.4 IMPERIALISM, 10th Grade Imperialism Inquiry, Do the Boxers Deserve a Bad Rap?)[4]

- **What was the Enlightenment and what were the Enlightenment writers' views on human rights?** Define Enlightenment and design a chart listing the major Enlightenment writers, their major works, a brief biography of where they were from, and their essential Enlightenment ideas expressed in their writings. (Formative Performance Task, 10th Grade Enlightenment and Revolutions Inquiry, How Did Reason Lead to Revolution?)[5]

It is extremely helpful to understand not just that students need to construct an explanation to respond to those questions, but that we have choices about what type of certain explanation that would best serve the content. This entails thinking about the social purpose in more detail; for example, if the purpose was to look at the factors that lead up to an event in the past, this explanation would look different from one in which we focused on the present-day consequences of a past event. Here are some of the major types listed with the social purpose and examples you might see in the curriculum (Table 2.1).

The type of explanation should match the social studies way of thinking, reasoning, and explaining best suited for the content. If our content is women's suffrage and we want our students to explain why there was opposition, the kind of reasoning we want them to do is one in which they identify and analyze the *factors* that contributed to the opposition, such as the divisions in roles at the time between men and women, with the women taking care of the home and the men the business life outside the home. The kind of explanation we would want them to use would be a *factorial* explanation.

Table 2.1 Types of Explanations in Social Studies

Types of explanation	Social purpose of explanation	Sample curricular context	Formats
Causal Explanation	Explain a phenomenon that involves an element of causality	What has caused the gender wage gap in the United States?	Poster
			Letter
		Determine the major causes of the Dust Bowl[6]	Blog
			Map
System Explanation	Explain how a system works in terms of the relationships between its parts	What is the relationship between the legislative, judicial, and executive branches of the US government?	Essay
			Digital documentary
			Debate
		If you wanted to change the constitution, what would you need to do?	Speech
			Social media post
			Billboard
			Meme
			Powerpoint
			Speech
			Infographics

(Continued)

Table 2.1 (Continued)

Types of explanation	Social purpose of explanation	Sample curricular context	Formats
Factorial Explanation	Explain the factors that contribute to a particular outcome	Why was there so much opposition to women's suffrage? What is causing the drought in the western United States? How did the Opium Wars create foreign influence in China and how did China react?	Factor, Factor, Factor → Outcome
Consequential Explanation	Explain the effects or consequences of a situation or event	Why are some people opposed to gerrymandering? How did slavery shape my state?[7]	Input → Consequence, Consequence, Consequence

Adapted from Coffin (2009) and Derewianka and Jones (2016).

Explanations

> ## 2.1* Try it out
> Look back at the vignette that starts this chapter. What type of explanation is Mr. Rodriguez looking for? Rewrite the assignment so that the genre and type of explanation are more clear. Choose a visual representation of the type of explanation you would present to students. See the answer key at the end of the chapter if you want a hint.
>
> *(Numbering 2.1, etc. corresponds with the Answer Key)

We are thinking that Mr. Rodriguez is looking for a consequential explanation. This type of explanation describes how a certain historical situation or geographical event led to one or more consequences. In writing a consequential explanation for Mr. Rodriguez, his students would choose an event related to Native American tribes and nations and explain the consequences of that event. Here is an example of a consequential explanation that Mr. Rodriguez was really happy with. Have a quick read and then we will walk you through an analysis where we make visible the moves the writer used to create this piece.

> ## The Consequences of the Boarding Schools on the Ho-Chunk People
>
> In Wisconsin in the late 1800s, many children of the Ho-Chunk nation were taken from their homes and sent away to boarding schools. The goal of these schools was assimilation, a political and social goal of the US government, designed to make the Native American children learn the language and culture of the white people. This had severe and lasting consequences on the Ho-Chunk community.
>
> One consequence these boarding schools had was a disconnection of the children from the cultural ways of the Ho-Chunk which was achieved through systemic repression of the Ho-Chunk culture with particular focus on appearance, farming practices, and spiritual traditions....
>
> The second consequence the boarding schools had on the Ho-Chunk was the loss of their language....
>
> (See Appendix for the Complete Text)

Explanations

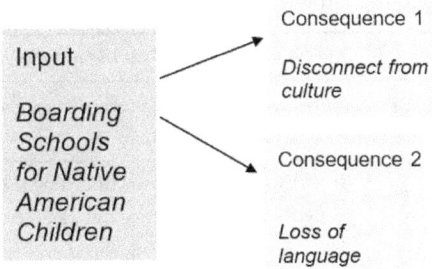

Figure 2.2 Input and consequences
Credit: Adapted from Coffin (2009) and Derewianka and Jones (2016)

The writer here chose the sending away of children to boarding schools as the event, or input that lead to two main consequences: One, the disconnection of children from their culture, and two, the loss of language (Figure 2.2).

This graphic makes clear what has happened (Boarding Schools) and what needs to be explained (how the input of the Boarding Schools led to the two consequences: Disconnection from their culture and the loss of language). Graphics like this are very useful in that they convey the disciplinary reasoning that underlies the explanation and makes clear what exactly needs explaining.

Once we have established what type of explanation we want our students to write, the next thing we need to do is think about the genre structure of that explanation. At face value, the genre structure looks like an outline, but it goes further in that the structure represents the purpose and function of each stage or paragraph. As we saw above, it is not enough to give an outline that goes, Introduction, Body Paragraph 1, 2, 3, Conclusion. Instead, each genre stage names the purpose, function, or "job" of each part. Once the jobs are established, the content can be mapped out to align with the stages (Table 2.2).

Next is to think about the content appropriate for the job of each genre stage. By job we mean purpose or function. Note that these jobs describe the content including the disciplinary reasoning. Later we will look at language used to realize this content. Consider the following table which names the stage and job on the left and then lists the content on the right. Notice how the writer of the outline thought through the job of each stage. For example, with the first stage they considered: What are the important pieces of information I would need to include to identify the historical situation? Then, for the second stage, they thought: How would I elaborate on the effects of this event? What details should I include that I can expand upon?

Explanations

Table 2.2 Genre Stages Aligned with Content

What were the consequences of the boarding schools on the Ho-Chunk people?	
Consequential explanation genre stages	Jot down your ideas for content for each section
I Input Job of this stage: Identify historical situation or event leading to change	The historical situation – Boarding schools for indigenous peoples • 1880s Wisconsin • the US government took children of many Indian nations and sent them away to boarding schools • Goal was assimilation – learn language and culture of white people • Focus – Ho-Chunk nation
II Consequence 1 Job of this stage: Elaborate on the effects of the event	Effects of the boarding school movement on Ho-Chunk (part 1) Big idea consequence–Ho-Chunk kids lost their culture: • forced to cut their hair • taught new ways of farming • had to give up their spiritual traditions
III Consequence 2 Job of this stage: Elaborate on the effects of the event	Effects of boarding school movement on Ho-Chunk (part 2) Big idea consequence – Ho-Chunk kids lost their Ho-Chunk language: • Forced to speak English only • Couldn't speak with their elders when they went back home eventually • Weren't able to learn about their own history and how to be a good member of their Ho-Chunk community
IV Reinforcement of consequences Job of this stage: Emphasize and/or evaluate consequences	Emphasize how bad the boarding school movement was for the Ho-Chunk people: • Kids couldn't belong to their communities when they went back • Wouldn't let the kids do things important to their culture – so kids forgot about it or ended up preferring white culture • Loss of language meant that kids couldn't be connected to their people Evaluate the consequences: This led to … • Loss of Ho-Chunk culture (only small numbers understand the culture today) • Loss of Ho-Chunk language (only small numbers of people can still speak the language)

When you give students an outline for their written assignments, try using the genre stages: Name them and state their jobs. What this does is build student awareness of writing each section to carry out a specific purpose. Once students understand what they are aiming to do in a section, or the job of the section, then they can think about how to do that job with content and language features.

> ## 2.2 Try it out
>
> Look back at the Consequential Explanation of the Ho-Chunk Text. How well does that text use language to express content that serves the functions/jobs identified in the genre stages in Table 2.2. See if you can map the jobs to the text. See Appendix for the whole text.

In this chapter, we focus on consequential explanations. As you move on to other types of explanations, consult the descriptions and graphic representations above to help you figure out what stages you would like your students to address in their explanations.

Teaching students how to plan their writing using genre stages and jobs for each stage will go a long way in improving students' writing. However, if we stop our writing instruction at this point, we have answered the *what* part of writing, but we still haven't addressed the *how* part of writing. For example, *how* do we use language to "emphasize and evaluate consequences" which is the job of the conclusion? How do we use language to express our content? What kinds of language features do we choose amongst? In the next section, we delve into the *how* by focusing on the language writers use when expressing their ideas in explanations.

Part 2: What Language Do We Need to Express Our Ideas? Language Features in Social Studies Explanations

In the section above, we looked at explanations at the genre level, studying the text-level characteristics and thinking about the functions of explanations, which are primarily to express cause and effect. Our mentor text is a specific type of cause-and-effect explanation, a consequential explanation. In this section, we will look at the language features occurring at the sentence, word, and phrase level of explanations that communicate cause and effect. We will go through each type of feature in detail and give you exercises to try out and ideas for your classroom. Our goal is to empower you to teach these features to your students. Most students will need your support in making these features visible and in understanding how they work to communicate the social studies content.

Before we get to the language features salient to the Consequential Explanation that respond to the prompt, What were the Consequences of the Boarding Schools on the Ho-Chunk People?, we will look at some language features common to many explanations.

Now, let's narrow down and focus on a group of features that expresses cause and effect, which are going to be necessary in order to express the content of our Consequential Explanation that responds to the prompt, What were the Consequences of the Boarding Schools on the Ho-Chunk People?

Table 2.3 Language Features Common to Explanations

Possible language features common to historical explanations
Discourse (Text and Paragraph) Dimension: • Causal connectives (as a result of, for that reason, as a consequence, because of this, therefore) **Sentence (and Word Phrase) Dimension:** • Simple past tense to express generalizations (the goal of these schools was assimilation) • Dependent clauses to connect causes and consequences (because the children had to cut their hair, learn new ways of farming, and a new religion, they ended up being disconnected from Ho-Chunk culture) • Passive voice to talk about the object undergoing the process (the children were taught that Ho-Chunk ways of farming were backward) or to hide agency (many children of the Ho-Chunk nation were taken from their homes and sent away to boarding schools) **Word Dimension:** • General, topic-specific, nonhuman participants, abstract nouns (consequence, assimilation, a political and social goal) • Noun groups carry a great deal of meaning though through adjectives (severe and lasting (consequences)) and prepositional phrases (from the cultural ways, from Ho-Chunk culture)

Brisk (2023); Derewianka and Jones (2023).

At the register level, the group of features in Table 2.3 fits into the metafunctions Field and Mode in the Trinocular Model of Register Figure in Chapter 1. Field refers to ideational meanings in particularly how we express and connect ideas. Mode refers to cohesion, or how we organize our thoughts across a piece of writing. While there are language features of Tenor, how we interact with our audience, also in Explanations, we are going to focus on Field and Mode here. In Chapter 3, we focus on Tenor.

Consider the following table (Table 2.4). The left-hand column identifies the function, purpose, or "job" of the language feature. In the middle is the technical term for the features, and on the right we illustrate the feature with examples from the text as well as some that are not in the text but we felt would be useful.

We now will go into each of these features in detail inviting you to deepen your understanding with examples for you to practice as well as suggestions for how you can draw attention to these features in your teaching. For each of this group of features that follows, we include an excerpt from our mentor text that illustrates that example. You can find the full text with features highlighted in the Appendix.

Language Features for Holding the Explanation Together to Create a Cohesive Essay

This group of features functions to manage the cohesion of the essay, in other words, to glue it together in a logical way. These are highlighted below in an excerpt from our Consequential Explanation.

Paragraph Openers

In Wisconsin in the late 1800s, many children of the Ho-Chunk nation were taken from their homes and sent away to boarding schools....

One consequence these boarding schools had was a disconnection....

The second consequence these boarding schools had on the Ho-Chunk was the loss of their language....

The consequence of sending Ho-Chunk children away to boarding school was a devastating loss of the Ho-Chunk culture and language.

Explanations

Table 2.4 Language Features to Express Cause and Effect

Metafunction	Job of the language feature	What it's called	Examples
Mode	Hold the explanation at the whole text level together to create a cohesive essay	Paragraph openers	One consequence …
	Organize the sentences within a paragraph	Text connectives	First, Second, Lastly
	Make cause-effect links	Text connectives showcasing cause-effect	Therefore, consequently, for this reason, as a result, hence, thus, as a consequence, accordingly, because of this, so, then, due to
		Verb groups	Led to, ended up, caused
		Noun groups	Consequences, effects, result
		Referring pronouns	This
		Causal clauses	I had to work late because my coworker called in sick
			My coworker calling in sick resulted in my having to work late
			By not allowing the children to practice their culture, the result was …
Field	Provide details about the causes and the effects	Extended noun groups	A devastating loss of the Ho-Chunk culture and language
	Condense activities and evaluations	Nominalizations	Assimilation, disconnection, removal

We use paragraph openers to start each paragraph for the purpose of organizing and connecting the paragraphs together in the essay. It's most effective when these are specific to the type of explanation. In the "The Consequences of the Boarding Schools on the Ho-Chunk People" text, the first paragraph opener sets the context, *In Wisconsin in the late 1800s*. The rest of paragraph openers include the word consequences, for example, *One consequence ... the second consequence ... the consequences*. Repeating consequence first, creates a cohesive text that is neatly glued together, and second, explicitly tells the reader that this is a consequential explanation. While this may seem straightforward, students may not have learned to strategically use paragraph openers to align with the purpose of their explanations. If this is the case, then the students' essays will not seem coherent, so it is important to teach students to pay attention to paragraph openers.

Something you can do in your classroom is to have students collect paragraph openers from model essays and readings. They can vandalize texts by switching out the paragraph openers for different ones. They can also make anchor charts with these paragraph openers to support their writing.

Language Features to Organize the Sentences within a Paragraph

Text Connectives

These are single words or groups of words, including *first, second, therefore, furthermore, in addition, for example, as a result*, and so on used to create logical connections between ideas. While paragraph openers provide a macro-level organization of a whole text and occur just at the beginning of paragraphs, text connectives occur within paragraphs and provide a microlevel organization. If you think of a piece of writing as a map, the text connectives are the signposts that tell the reader which way to go next.

> One consequence these boarding schools had was a disconnection of the children from the cultural ways of the Ho-Chunk, which was achieved through systemic repression of the Ho-Chunk culture with particular focus on appearance, farming practices, and spiritual traditions. First, to make the Ho-Chunk children look more like white

Explanations

> people, the teachers cut off the children's long hair. This was cruel because long hair was an intrinsic part of the children's identity as Ho-Chunk. Second, the children were taught that Ho-Chunk ways of farming were backward and forced to learn new ways of farming. The third example ...

You are no doubt most familiar with text connectives that sequence ideas. Those are the ones we highlighted in the excerpt above: *one ... first ... second ... the third example....* These sequencing text connectives are not difficult to teach as they correspond directly to numbering and outlining that students are likely used to. There is another set of text connectives, however, that we need to showcase cause-and-effect relationships. Study the following excerpt:

> The second consequence the boarding schools had on the Ho-Chunk was the loss of their language. At school, the children had to speak English. They were not allowed to speak Ho-Chunk language at all. As a result, there was a lot of language loss that had the tragic effect of the children not being able to understand and not being able to connect with their elders when they eventually were allowed to return to their communities. Since they could not communicate with their elders, the children were unable to participate in the cultural practice of using stories to teach the children about their history and how to be a good member of the community.

Language to Make Cause-and-Effect Links

Cause and effect is critical as a type of disciplinary meaning in social studies and is often the main focus in explanations. As you saw in Table 2.3, we called out six ways we use language strategically to make cause-and-effect links. One way is with text connectives that express cause and effect. In the excerpt above, *as a result* expresses cause and effect by connecting the cause (*they were not allowed to speak Ho-Chunk language*) with the effect (*there was a lot of language loss which had the tragic effect ...*). *Since* also expresses cause and effect by connecting the cause (*they could not communicate with their elders*) to the effect (*the children were unable to participate ...*).

Text Connectives can fulfill a variety of functions as you will see here (Table 2.5).

Something you can do in your classroom is to create a bank of text connectives. Divide them into Text Connectives Sequencing Ideas (first, second, finally, etc.) and Text Connectives Showcasing Cause-effect (so, then, therefore, etc.).

Another thing you could do is invite students to replace the text connectives in the mentor text and discuss how that changes the meaning. Example: Invite the students to replace *as a result* with *and*. Ask them: *How*

Table 2.5 Text Connectives

Clarifying		Showcasing cause/result	
in other words	in particular	so	as a result
for example	in fact	then	for that reason
for instance	that is	therefore	due to
to be more precise	to illustrate	as a consequence/ consequently	accordingly because of this
Indicating time		*Sequencing ideas*	
then	soon	first(ly)/first of all	to summarize/ sum up
next	after a while		
afterward	later	to start with/to begin	finally/a final point
at the same time	previously		
in the end	until then	second, third, fourth	in conclusion
finally		at this point	given the above points
		briefly	
Adding information		*Condition/concession*	
in addition	above all	in that case	even so
also	as well	on the other hand	despite this
furthermore	moreover	otherwise	at least
and besides	similarly/equally	on the contrary	besides
along with	in the same way	however	though
		anyhow/anyway	yet
		nevertheless	despite this

Humphrey et al. (2012, p. 136)

Explanations

does that change the meaning? (and adds on information, but it doesn't tell us what caused what).

Referring Pronoun "this"

The pronoun "this" is often used in explanations to condense information in a cause-and-effect sequence. In this example from the text, "this" is used to refer to the entire chunk of information that is in italics: *At school, the children had to speak English. They were not allowed to speak Ho-Chunk language at all.* <u>This</u> resulted in language loss …

Understanding how "this" is used is important both for comprehension of cause-and-effect sequences and in writing them. In our experience, in reading, students typically need support in identifying exactly what "this" refers to. With writing, students need practice using "this" to make their writing cohesive and efficient.

Cause-and-Effect Subordinate Clauses

These are clauses that signal that something happened that resulted in an effect on something else. In other words, these clauses are the bread and butter of expressing cause-and-effect links. Because these are so important, we will spend a little time on them.

Let's start by listing some events that would have an impact on something else:

I went to bed late.
I didn't study for the test.
I forgot to fill the car up with gas.

Now let's think of the potential impacts of each of those events:

Events	Impact
I went to bed late	I felt tired and unproductive the next day
I didn't study for the test	I failed the test
I forgot to fill the car up with gas	I ran out of gas

In English, we can express these ideas by juxtaposing the sentences; for example, *I forgot to fill the car up with gas. I ran out of gas.* However, in order to express the relationship of one idea causing another in the clearest and most impactful way, we need the causal clause structure. There are two typical choices we have for this:

Causal Structure Choice 1: Event + Cause-effect link + Impact
Causal Structure Choice 2: Impact + Cause-effect link + Event

2.3 Try it out

2.3 Event	Cause-effect links	Impact
I went to bed late	so	I felt tired and unproductive the next day
I didn't study for my test		
I forgot to fill the car up with gas		
I didn't vote		
The Ho-Chunk children couldn't communicate with their elders		

Now try filling in the table with the "events" and the "impacts" reversed. Can you still use the same subordinate conjunctions?

2.4 Try it out

2.4 Impact	Specific Words signaling the cause-effect link (subordinate conjunctions)	Event
I felt tired and productive the next day	because	I went to bed late
		I didn't study for my test
		I forgot to fill the car up with gas
		I didn't vote
		The Ho-Chunk children couldn't communicate with their elders

Explanations

Another way to conceptualize these cause-and-effect links that may be helpful for your students is to ask *why* questions to establish what is causing what. For example:

I went to bed early – **Why?** I was tired.
The children were unable to participate in the cultural practice of using stories – **Why?** They couldn't communicate with their elders.

It is tricky to start with a consequence or impact and work backward to figure out the event that caused it. In addition to using tables like the ones above with your students, you can also support them with consequential explanations by teaching them to ask **why** questions. Students can generate consequences from their lives, and as a class you can fill in a table like this.

What is something you had to do over the weekend that you didn't want to do?

2.5 Try it out

2.5 Impact/ Consequence	(why?)	Specific words signaling the cause-effect link (subordinate conjunctions)	Event
I had to babysit last minute		because	my mom had to work
I had to work late		because	my coworker didn't show up

Language to Provide Details about the Causes and the Effects

Extended Noun Groups to Provide Detail

Next we move on from the cause-and-effect links to ways we add detail about the causes and effects; this is done primarily through the noun groups (de Oliveira, 2010). As you may remember from elementary school, a noun is a "person, place, or thing." But what is the job of a noun? How does it provide details? If verbs describe *what is happening*, nouns describe *who* or *what*. In explanations, noun groups are where we put in the crucial details that express our ideas that have to do with the *who* and *what*. English allows us to extend noun groups indefinitely so that we can provide rich and detailed information. As students progress through school, the noun groups they need to produce and comprehend become longer and longer, and we may refer to the texts with these long noun groups as dense. It is not uncommon in academic writing in middle and high school to have noun groups with 15–20 words in them, like the ones in our mentor text. These extended noun groups can be difficult for students to unpack and comprehend and for writers to know how to build them. An important part of teaching explanations is, therefore, going to be to teach students how to develop extended noun groups for writing and how to unpack extended noun groups so that they comprehend the text.

Consider this next example:

> One consequence schools had was children lost their culture. They weren't allowed to engage in traditions.

These sentences make sense, but there are missed opportunities here to extend the underlined nouns to provide detail and questions the reader would have, for example, which schools, what kinds of schools? The resulting noun group that answers these questions could be, *these boarding schools*, but we could also expand this even more, packing even more details:

Which?	How many?	What are they like?	What kind are they?	What?
These	hundreds of	horrific	boarding	schools

We can do the same with *traditions*. Try this one out:

2.6 Try it out

2.6 Which?	How many?	What are they like?	What kind are they?	What?
				traditions

Explanations

There are other questions we could ask about the noun to pack in even more detail. We can ask *where?* and *how?* We often use prepositional phrases to add these details:

Where? *In Wisconsin, throughout the country*
How? *with particular focus on appearance, farming practices, and spiritual traditions.*

Last, but certainly not least, we can expand noun groups with relative clauses. As students move through the grades and into high school, the disciplinary literacy expectations for social studies demand that writers condense information using resources including embedded clauses. One particular type of embedded clause that students need to know how to comprehend and produce is a relative clause. These clauses typically begin with a relative pronoun, for example, **that, which, who, was, where**. Importantly, these relative clauses contain a verb. Embedding clauses into noun groups condenses information and allows us to pack in the details we need in our explanations. These can function to answer questions like *what's it like?*, *which?*, *what kind*, and *what else?* Here is an example, the relative clause is underlined and the relative pronoun is in bold:

My friend, **who** <u>lives in Virginia</u>, is coming to visit.

There are a lot of restrictions on how you can use relative clauses, the main restriction being that the clause cannot hang out on its own. So you can't have a sentence like this: **Who lives in Virginia.* Nor could you skip verb inside the clause about what the friend is doing like this: **My friend who in Virginia is coming to visit.*

You *can*, however, remove the clause and end up with a complete sentence:

My friend is coming to visit.

Try writing a different sentence with a relative clause here:

2.7 Try it out

My friend, _____, is _____.
    Relative clause

Students who are new to writing explanations will often express their ideas in a series of choppy sentences, such as the ones here:

> There were government officials. They were unethical. They sent the Ho-Chunk children away. They sent them to Boarding Schools.

While these ideas are clear and relevant, this is not an efficient way to package information. Try condensing the four sentences above into one with a relative clause.

2.8 Try it out

> There were government officials. They were unethical. They sent the Ho-Chunk children away. They sent them to Boarding Schools.

Our mentor text has many extended noun groups that serve to pack in detail. Here are two examples from the Ho-Chunk text:

Extended noun group using a relative clause	
What?	What else?
language loss	which had the tragic effect of the children not being able to understand and not being able to connect with their elders when they eventually were allowed to return to their communities.

Extended noun group using a prepositional phrase and a relative clause		
What	What kind? (prepositional phrase)	What else? (relative clause)
a disconnection	of the children from the cultural ways of the Ho-Chunk	which was achieved through systemic repression of the Ho-Chunk culture with particular focus on appearance, farming practices, and spiritual traditions

Those examples are what we would call dense text. Students need support with both unpacking and repackaging text like this. To support your students in writing extended noun groups, consider the following ideas:

Explanations

In your classroom, you could challenge students to a game in which they take a noun and expand it as much as they can. We recommend starting with a common noun like a dog, then switching over to a noun from your content. Winner has the longest noun group.

You could list a series of probe questions in an anchor chart which could include the following: which?, how many?, what like?, what type?, whose?, how?, what kind?, what for?, with what?

You could also provide students with a table like the one below:

Which?	How many?	What's it like?	Who or what?	What else?
Those	two	unethical	government officials	who were responsible for sending off the Ho-Chunk children to the Boarding schools

Think for a moment, how could you use this way of asking probe questions to help students with their reading? How could you unpack a dense sentence for them?

Here is an example of how you might do that:

Sentence	As a result, there was a lot of language loss, which had the tragic effect of the children not being able to understand and not being able to connect with their elders when they eventually were allowed to return to their communities
Unpacked	there was a lot of language loss (which loss?) which had the tragic effect (What effect?) of the children not being able to understand (And what other effect?) not being able to connect with their elders (when?) when they eventually were allowed to return (where?) to their communities

Incidentally, this way of looking at text makes visible the dialogue that underlies the text. Helping students to understand this is crucial in supporting their comprehension as it illustrates how ideas within a sentence are connected. We will go into more detail on this in Chapter 5.

Language to Condense Activities and Evaluations: Nominalizations

Nominalizations are when we take action words or entire clauses and transform them into nouns, often, but not always, adding *-tion* to the verb:

Action word (verb)	Nominalization (noun)
Disconnect	Disconnection
Assimilate	Assimilation
Remove	Removal

There are particular reasons why we would want to use nominalization in social studies explanations. Often in historical texts, the human agency is hidden and the consequences of actions are foregrounded. For example,

> The **removal** of the Ho-chunk people from their native lands led to devastating consequences.

In the sentence above, the human agency is hidden. The text doesn't say who removed them. The sentence emphasizes the removal of the Ho-Chunk people, not who did the action. It is achieved through nominalization. The word "removal" is a nominalized form of the verb "to remove". This sentence illustrates that human agency can be hidden through nominalization.

In the previous section, we discussed how to expand noun phrases. Nominalization, does the opposite, enabling us to take whole chunks of meaning and pack them into one word.

Chunk of meaning (clauses)	Condensing meaning with nominalization
When the Ho-Chunk people were removed	the removal of the Ho-Chunk
When the people's language was lost	language loss

Nominalization is a common language feature in academic writing for social studies because it enables writers to put a lot of content into the sentence and to organize the content based on what the author feels is most important. As mentioned above, the agency of who did what to whom gets removed when we nominalize. Note how the "people" comes out when we nominalize the clauses. Play around with nominalization here:

Explanations

2.9 Try it out

2.9 Action word (verb)	Nominalization (noun)
Solve	
	Reaction
Interfere	
Decide	

2.10 Try it out

2.10 Chunk of meaning (clauses)	Condensing meaning with nominalization
They distributed the pizzas to everyone in a fair way	
	The analysis came back guilty
The parties agreed to reach a plea deal	

In your classroom you can use the tables above to support students' practice in nominalization. Students can also hunt for examples of nominalization in their texts.

Summary

In this chapter, we described the nature of language in social studies by focusing on some of the explaining genres. A key part of social studies reasoning is concerned with explaining why something happened in the past for the purpose of informing the present and the future. We identified several kinds of explanations that are important to social studies, such as causal, sequential, systems, factorial, and consequential. We explained how explanations are organized at the genre level and used the metaphor of jobs to describe the purpose or function of each section of an explanation. We emphasized the importance of explicitly teaching students to think about their writing in this way. We then zoomed in to the word, phrase, clause, and sentence level to examine how we create cause-and-effect meaning using certain language features. Our goal in this chapter was to make visible for you both these genre features and language features to empower you to be able to teach these to your students. In the next chapter, we'll be looking at different types of arguments in social studies at the genre and register level.

Vignette: Reprisal

At the beginning of the chapter we asked you to imagine a different way of presenting an assignment to students, one that made the language demands visible. Here is Mr. Rodriguez's white board and his dialogue with the students. Compare this with the vignette that opened the chapter. How does this version promote equitable achievement? (Figure 2.3):

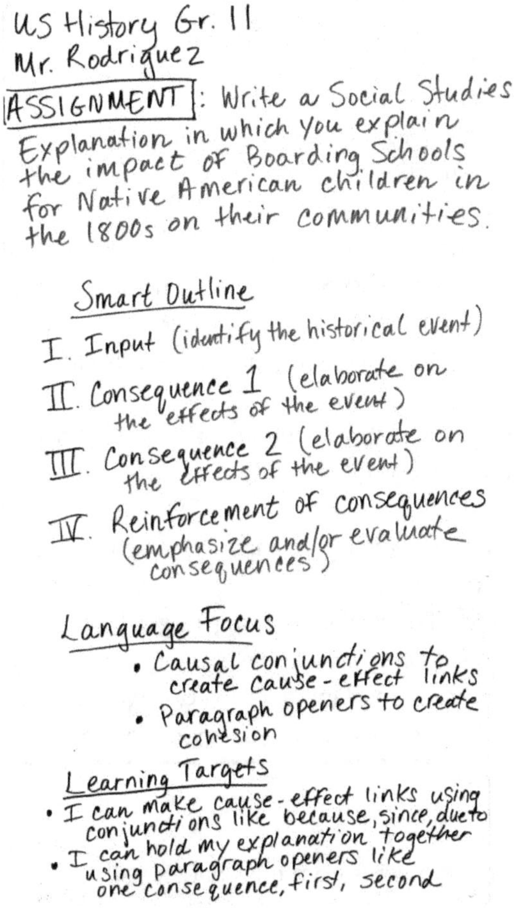

> US History Gr. 11
> Mr. Rodriguez
> ASSIGNMENT: Write a Social Studies Explanation in which you explain the impact of Boarding Schools for Native American children in the 1800s on their communities.
>
> Smart Outline
> I. Input (identify the historical event)
> II. Consequence 1 (elaborate on the effects of the event)
> III. Consequence 2 (elaborate on the effects of the event)
> IV. Reinforcement of consequences (emphasize and/or evaluate consequences)
>
> Language Focus
> • Causal conjunctions to create cause-effect links
> • Paragraph openers to create cohesion
>
> Learning Targets
> • I can make cause-effect links using conjunctions like because, since, due to
> • I can hold my explanation together using paragraph openers like one consequence, first, second

Figure 2.3 Mr. Rodriquez's whiteboard

Explanations

T: Today I want you to plan out your Consequential Explanation on the topic we have been studying, the Boarding School Movement in the 1800s in the US. Here is a copy of the model text for a Consequential Explanation that we analyzed. You are also going to want to look at the Consequential Explanation you wrote in your groups. The explanation you will write will be modeled after both of those texts.

Before you get started let's look at our model text and quickly remind ourselves of language features we learned about that we need to include when writing explanations in social studies. Maria, can you start us out, what is one of the language features we need to include?

Maria: Paragraph openers

T: That's right, can you add on to that, what job do the paragraph openers do for us?

Maria: Help us glue our essay together

T: Exactly, what else? Tony?

Tony: Causal conjunctions

T: Like what?

Tony: Because, since, due to

Teacher: Yes, who can add on to what Tony said, what job do these causal conjunctions do for us in our explanations?

Bella: We can use them to create our cause-and-effect links.

T: Ok, tell us more.

Bella: Like we can say that if something happened, it happened because something caused it.

T: Yes.

T: Can I get someone to read the Language Focus and Learning Targets for today?

Ss: [Read Language Focus and Learning Targets]

T: Thank you. Now, does anyone have any questions or are you ready to get to work on planning? No? Ok, we will save five minutes at the end of class to have you reflect on the learning targets.

Now, try out the concepts from this chapter with your own curriculum:

2.11 Try it out

Choose 2–3 of your favorite (or imagined) explanation assignments. Use the table below.

1. Write the assignments in the column, "curricular context."
2. Think about their social purpose and genre. Try to be specific about the genre, what type of explanation is it? Causal? Systems? Factorial? Consequential?
3. Next think about the text structure that would fulfill the social purpose of the assignment. If you taught this assignment before, you may already have an outline that you used; you can put that in the table. Or, if it's a new assignment, you can use one of the possible text structures from the above tables. Below is a table to help you get started. What's foregrounded in a text? If it's factors, then it's a factorial explanation, but if it's consequences, then it's consequential.

Genre	Social purpose	Curricular context (your assignment)	Possible text structure (outline)
Consequential	Explain the effects or consequences of a situation or event	How did slavery shape my state? "How did sugar feed slavery?" students explore the environmental, economic, and social consequences of increased sugar production	• Input: Identify historical situation or event leading to change • Consequence 1, 2, 3: Elaborate the effects of consequence of situation or event • Reinforcement of consequences: Emphasize and/or evaluate consequences

Notes

1   https://c3teachers.org/inquiries/
2   https://c3teachers.org/inquiries/bananas/
3   https://c3teachers.org/inquiries/dust-bowl/
4   https://c3teachers.org/inquiries/imperialism/
5   https://c3teachers.org/inquiries/enlightenment-and-revolutions/
6   https://c3teachers.org/inquiries/dust-bowl/
7   https://c3teachers.org/inquiries/slavery-shape-state/

References

Brisk, M. (2023). *Engaging students in academic literacies: SFL genre pedagogy for K-8 classrooms* (2nd ed.). Routledge.

Coffin, C. (2009). *Historical discourse. The language of time, cause and evaluation*. Bloomsbury.

de Oliveira, L. C. (2010). Nouns in history: Packaging information, expanding explanations, and structuring reasoning. *The History Teacher, 43*(2), 191–203. http://www.jstor.org/stable/40543286

de Oliveira, L. C., & Obenchain, K. (2019). *Teaching history and social studies to English language learners: Preparing pre-service and in-service teachers*. Palgrave MacMillan.

Derewianka, B., & Jones, P. (2023). *Teaching language in context* (3rd ed.). Oxford University Press.

Humphrey, S., Droga, L., & Feez, S. (2012). *Grammar and meaning*. PETAA.

National Council for the Social Studies Standards. (n.d.). College, Career, and Civics (C3) Framework for Social Studies. https://www.socialstudies.org/standards/c3

Schleppegrell, M. (2004). *The language of schooling. A functional linguistics perspective*. Laurence Earlbaum Publishers.

Chapter 2 Appendix

Consequential Explanation: Full Text Version

The Consequences of the Boarding Schools on the Ho-Chunk People

In Wisconsin in the late 1800s, many children of the Ho-Chunk nation were taken from their homes and sent away to boarding schools. The goal of these schools was assimilation, a political and social goal of the US government, designed to make the Native American children learn the language and culture of the white people. This had severe and lasting consequences on the Ho-Chunk community.

One consequence these boarding schools had was a disconnection of the children from the cultural ways of the Ho-Chunk, which was achieved through systemic repression of the Ho-Chunk culture with particular focus on appearance, farming practices, and spiritual traditions. First, to make the Ho-Chunk children look more like white people, the teachers cut off the children's long hair. This was cruel because long hair was an intrinsic part of the children's identity as Ho-Chunk. Second, the children were taught that Ho-Chunk ways of farming were backward and forced to learn new ways of farming. The third example of repressing culture was with spiritual traditions. The children were taught Western religion in school. They were not allowed to practice Ho-Chunk spiritual traditions. Because the children had to cut their hair, learn new ways of farming, and a new religion, they ended up being disconnected from Ho-Chunk culture.

The second consequence the boarding schools had on the Ho-Chunk was the loss of their language. At school, the children had to speak English. They were not allowed to speak Ho-Chunk language at all. As a result, there was a lot of language loss, which had the tragic effect of the children not being able to understand and not being able to connect with their elders when they eventually were allowed to return to their communities. Since they could not communicate with their elders, the children were unable to

Explanations

participate in the cultural practice of using stories to teach the children about their history and how to be a good member of the community.

The consequence of sending Ho-Chunk children away to boarding school was a devastating loss of the Ho-Chunk culture and language. By not allowing the children to practice their culture, the result was the children forgot the culture or ended up preferring the white culture. By not allowing the children to speak Ho-Chunk language, the result was the children couldn't speak to or understand their elders, so they lost that connection to their historical traditions. Therefore, over time, the Ho-Chunk language was used by fewer and fewer children, and because of this, fewer adults.

Full Text Analysis of Language Features in Context

The Consequences of the Boarding Schools on the Ho-Chunk People

In Wisconsin in the late 1800s, many children of the Ho-Chunk nation were taken from their homes and sent away to boarding schools. The goal of these schools was <u>assimilation</u>, a political and social goal of the US government, designed to make the native American children learn the language and culture of the white people. (This) had severe and lasting consequences on the Ho-Chunk community.

One consequence these boarding schools had was a <u>disconnection of the children from the cultural ways of the Ho-Chunk, which was achieved through systemic repression of the Ho-Chunk culture with particular focus on appearance, farming practices, and spiritual traditions.</u> **First,** to make the Ho-Chunk children look more like white people, the teachers cut off the children's long hair. (This) was cruel because long hair was an intrinsic part of the children's identity as Ho-Chunk. **Second,** the children were taught that Ho-Chunk ways of farming were backward and forced to learn new ways of farming. **The third example** of repressing culture was with spiritual traditions. The children were taught Western religion in school. They were not allowed to practice <u>Ho-Chunk spiritual traditions</u>. <u>Because the children had to cut their hair, learn new ways of farming, and a new religion,</u> they ended up being disconnected from Ho-Chunk culture.

The second consequence the boarding schools had on the Ho-Chunk was the loss of their language. At school, the children had to speak English. They were not allowed to speak Ho-Chunk language at all. **As a result**, there was a lot of language loss, which had the tragic effect of the children not being able to understand and not being able to connect with their elders when they eventually were allowed to return to their communities. **<u>Since</u>** <u>they could not communicate with their elders,</u> the children were unable to participate in the cultural practice of using stories to teach the children about their history and how to be a good member of the community.

The consequence of sending Ho-Chunk children away to boarding school was a devastating loss of the Ho-Chunk culture and language. <u>By not allowing the children to practice their culture</u>, the result was the children forgot the culture or ended up preferring the white culture. <u>By not allowing the children to speak Ho-Chunk language,</u> the result was the children couldn't speak to or understand their elders, so they lost that connection to their historical traditions. **Therefore,** over time, the Ho-Chunk language was used by fewer and fewer children, and because of (this), fewer adults.

Key:
Paragraph Openers
Text Connectives
<u>Clauses expressing cause-effect links (Causal clauses)</u>
Causal language (verbs, nouns, phrases)
(Referring pronoun this)
<u>Extended noun groups</u>
Complex sentences with dependent clauses (<u>dependent clauses underlined</u>)
<u>Nominalizations</u>

Explanations

Chapter 2 Answer Key

2.1 Genre – Explanation: Consequential. "Write a consequential explanation in which you explain the effects or consequences of the Boarding School Movement on the Native American community."

2.2

Genre stage (and purpose)	Text
Input (identify historical situation or event leading to change)	In Wisconsin in the late 1800s, many children of the Ho-Chunk nation were taken from their homes and sent away to boarding schools. The goal of these schools was assimilation, a political and social goal of the US government, designed to make the native American children learn the language and culture of the white people. This had severe and lasting consequences on the Ho-Chunk community.
Consequence 1 (elaborate on the effects of the event)	One consequence these boarding schools had was a disconnection of the children from the cultural ways of the Ho-Chunk, which was achieved through systemic repression of the Ho-Chunk culture with particular focus on appearance, farming practices, and spiritual traditions. First, to make the Ho-Chunk children look more like white people, the teachers cut off the children's long hair. This was cruel because long hair was an intrinsic part of the children's identity as Ho-Chunk. Second, the children were taught that Ho-Chunk ways of farming were backward and forced to learn new ways of farming. The third example of repressing culture was with spiritual traditions. The children were taught Western religion in school. They were not allowed to practice Ho-Chunk spiritual traditions. Because the children had to cut their hair, learn new ways of farming, and a new religion, they ended up being disconnected from Ho-Chunk culture.
Consequence 2 (elaborate on the effects of the event)	The second consequence the boarding schools had on the Ho-Chunk was the loss of their language. At school, the children had to speak English. They were not allowed to speak Ho-Chunk language at all. This resulted in language loss, which had the tragic effect of the children not being able to understand and not being able to

(Continued)

Explanations

Genre stage (and purpose)	Text
	connect with their elders when they eventually were allowed to return to their communities. Since they could not communicate with their elders, the children were unable to participate in the cultural practice of using stories to teach the children about their history and how to be a good member of the community.
Reinforcement of consequences (emphasize and/ or evaluate consequences)	The consequence of sending Ho-Chunk children away to boarding school was a devastating loss of the Ho-Chunk culture and language. By not allowing the children to practice their culture, the result was the children forgot the culture or ended up preferring the white culture. By not allowing the children to speak Ho-Chunk language, the result was the children couldn't speak to or understand their elders, so they lost that connection to their historical traditions. Therefore, over time, the Ho-Chunk language was used by fewer and fewer children, and because of this, fewer adults.

2.3 Event	Cause-effect links	Impact
I went to bed late	so	I felt tired and unproductive the next day.
I didn't study for my test	as a result	I failed.
I forgot to fill the car up with gas	not surprisingly	I ran out of gas on the freeway.
I didn't vote	because of that	I didn't exercise my democratic privilege.
The Ho-Chunk children couldn't communicate with their elders	so	They lost connection with their grandparents.

2.4 Impact	Specific words signaling the cause-effect link (subordinate conjunctions)	Event
I felt tired and productive the next day	because	I went to bed late.
I failed	since	I didn't study for my test.

(Continued)

Explanations

2.4 Impact	Specific words signaling the cause-effect link (subordinate conjunctions)	Event
I ran out of gas on the freeway	because	I forgot to fill the car up with gas.
I didn't exercise my democratic privilege	because	I didn't vote.
They lost connection with their grandparents	as a result of the fact	The Ho-Chunk children couldn't communicate with their elders.

2.5 Impact/ Consequence	(why?)	Specific words signaling the cause-effect link (subordinate conjunctions)	Event
I had to babysit last minute		because	My mom had to work.
I had to work late		because	My coworker didn't show up.
I was late to class		because	My alarm didn't go off.
I lost my phone		because	It fell out of my pocket.
I didn't have any clean clothes		because	I didn't have time to do laundry.

2.6 Which?	How many?	What are they like?	What kind are they?	What?
These	many	ancient	Spiritual	traditions

2.7

My friend, *who I went to high school with*, is meeting me for coffee.
    Relative clause

2.8

There were government officials. They were unethical. They sent the Ho-Chunk children away. They sent them to Boarding Schools.

    They were the unethical government officials <u>who were responsible for sending off the Ho-Chunk children to the Boarding schools.</u>

Explanations

2.9 Action word (verb)	Nominalization (noun)
Solve	Solution
React	Reaction
Interfere	Interference
Decide	Decision

2.10 Chunk of meaning (clauses)	Condensing meaning with nominalization
They distributed the pizzas to everyone in a fair way	The *distribution* of the pizzas was fair
The court analyzed the issue and concluded the defendant was guilty	The *analysis* came back guilty
The parties agreed to reach a plea deal	The *agreement* was a plea deal

2.11 Genre	Social purpose	Curricular context (your assignment)	Possible text structure (outline)
Consequential	Explain the effects or consequences of a situation or event	How did slavery shape my state? "How did sugar feed slavery?" students explore the environmental, economic, and social consequences of increased sugar production	• Input: Identify historical situation or event leading to change • Consequence 1, 2, 3: Elaborate the effects of consequence of situation or event • Reinforcement of consequences: Emphasize and/or evaluate consequences
System	Explain how a system works in terms of the relationships between its parts	What is the relationship between the legislative, judicial, and executive branches of the US government? If you wanted to change the constitution, what would you need to do?	Element 1 Function Element 2 Function

For more ideas for 2.11, see Table 2.1.

What Is the Nature of Language of Arguments in Social Studies?

What Do We Mean by Argue?

Vignette:

Ms. Beatty, Political Science, Grade 9

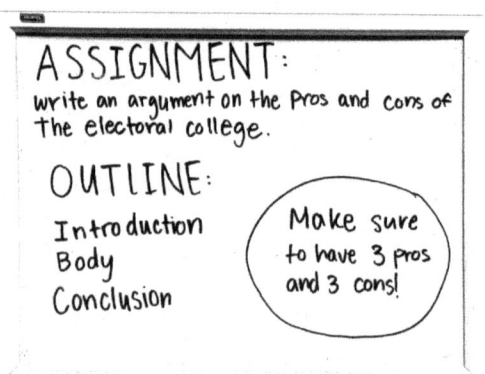

Figure 3.1 Ms. Beatty's writing on the board (before)

T: We've been talking a lot about the electoral college, you've done the research, reviewed multiple sources for both sides, and it's time to write an essay.
S: Essay, essay, essay, not another essay!
T: You're gonna thank me later. Writing will help you really clarify what you think you know.

DOI: 10.4324/9781003302711-3

S1: Yeah, we know that you don't win the presidency by a popular vote. Remember what happened to Hillary in 2016? She won by 2.3 million votes! This whole electoral college is so unfair. My mother is still mad about it.

S2: It may seem unfair but imagine if we had to do a recount! Let's count up all 200 million ballots just to double check! In the electoral college you just count the elector's votes, I could do that in my math class!

T: Hey, you two are having a great discussion! As you made it clear, there are pros and cons to this system and guess what, you are going to write about both sides. And because you can talk about it, it means you can write about it. Here's your rubric. You've written argument essays before, this shouldn't be that hard.

What Does It Look Like When We Don't Make Language Visible?

This is a typical classroom scenario in which the teacher, Ms. Beatty, teaches a unit on U.S. politics, specifically presidential elections. Ms. Beatty is a new social studies teacher and is passionate about teaching political science. But attending to writing in social studies is not something her pre-service teaching program addressed. Teaching writing was the job of the English Language Arts teacher. Ms. Beatty was trained in how to teach content or the subject matter of this deep and multidimensional discipline, not writing. So, Mrs. Beatty does not know much about the nuances of different kinds of arguments and how to teach the language of argumentation. When she was a student, her teachers told her, "Because you talk about it, it means you can write about it" and because writing was easy for her, she also assumed that it is true for her students. She's not alone in this assumption that if students did their research, and can discuss the topic, then they are ready to write about it.

Argument writing is challenging to native English speakers, let alone English language learners. Students need to know how to structure their arguments, how to appeal to the audience, and how to substantiate their claims with evidence. In this chapter, we are going to illustrate the language of argumentation in the context of a pros and cons argument genre. While it is typical for teachers to teach different kinds of sources to support their positions while teaching arguments, often, the language for doing this is not made visible. How, for example, do you use language resources for writing arguments with authority? What is the language for supporting claims with evidence in ways that are credible and appropriate to the audience? In order to make this visible for her students, Ms. Beatty needs to teach explicit lessons on how we use language features, for example to make a claim in a neutral way and how to present our position in a balanced less polarized approach.

How do we get from this vignette to a language-focused way of teaching social studies in a way that makes the language students need visible? Like we mentioned in Chapter 2, we start by attending to the genre. We need to be very clear about what genre we are asking our students to comprehend and produce. As you read in Chapter 2, in social studies, the main genres are explanations and arguments (Coffin, 2009; de Oliveira & Obenchain, 2019; Schleppegrell, 2004). This chapter will focus on arguments.

Purpose

This chapter is going to review what the C3 framework says about the genre of argumentation and then focus on language features that will help you talk to your students about the language they need to do the work of argumentation for the social studies you teach. In addition, it is going to show you how to help your students expand the meanings they make and ultimately expand their social studies linguistic repertoire.

Part 1: What Is Argumentation in Social Studies as Defined by the C3 Framework?

First, let's think about the nature of social studies arguments and what the College, Career, and Civics (C3) framework says about teaching argumentation. The C3 framework for States' Social Studies Standards describes arguments as

> in contrast to opinions and explanations, argumentation involves the ability to understand source-to-evidence relationship. That relationship emphasizes

the development of claims and counterclaims and the purposeful selection of evidence in support of those claims.

(C3 Framework, p. 55)

This process involves "gathering and evaluating sources" (Dimension 3 of C3 Framework, p. 54) as well as "constructing arguments using precise and knowledgeable claims, with evidence from multiple sources, while acknowledging strengths and evidentiary weakness" (p. 60). This is the nuts and bolts of our social studies disciplinary literacy.

Let's go back to our vignette now that we have reviewed C3 expectations for argumentation and compare what happened in her classroom and explore what else is might be missing that would promote student success. Ms. Beatty takes the students through the inquiry process by supporting students questioning and analysis, researching and weighing evidence, discussing and reasoning together about the issue. I am sure we could agree that this is exactly what we want to happen in our social studies classrooms. However, at the end, she gives them an argument writing assignment by telling them "If you can talk about it, you can write about it." She connects the ability to discuss with the ability to write. What is missing is explicit and sustained instruction in social studies literacy practices and systematic teaching of the language features of the argument genre. As you have read, most of our students need this critical component of explicit and systematic teaching of language of argumentation.

Part 2. Genre. What Are the Different Kinds of Arguments That Are Important to Social Studies?

To discover what kinds of arguments exist in social studies, let's take a look at a few examples from the C3 Inquiry Hub of sample inquiry units.[1] They all require that students will construct an argument.

- **Do we need the Electoral College?** Construct an argument (e.g., detailed outline, poster, essay) that discusses the compelling question using specific claims and relevant evidence from both historic and current sources while acknowledging competing views.[2]

- **Should the right to vote be protected in the Constitution?** Construct an argument (e.g., detailed outline, poster, essay) that responds to the compelling questions using specific claims and relevant evidence from sources while acknowledging competing views.[3]
- **Does money matter in political campaigns?** Construct an argument (e.g., detailed outline, poster, essay) that addresses the compelling question using specific claims and relevant evidence from contemporary sources while acknowledging competing perspectives.[4]

While the expectation to construct an argument is clear, what kind of argument is not. Furthermore, the way these inquiries are framed could be confusing. For example, "detailed outline, poster, essay" are not types of arguments, but formats that the writer could present their ideas. It is important to point this out to students. Additionally, while the inquiries hint at what the argument should entail, e.g., "discusses the compelling question using specific claims and relevant evidence from both historic and current sources while acknowledging competing views", we need to go further and dig into the question of what exactly do we mean by argument. For example, Is the purpose to challenge a popular position on a topic? Or is it to argue for a particular interpretation without necessarily recognizing alternative perspectives? Those two purposes will result in two different kinds of arguments.

It helps to focus on the social purpose of the arguments and make distinctions from that perspective (Coffin, 2009; Schleppegrell, 2004; Read.Inquire.Write) (Table 3.1).

Thinking about the different purposes of arguments will help you make this visible to students. Social studies argumentation gives students opportunities to consider social issues from multiple perspectives by weighing evidence and drawing conclusions. The products resulting from those conclusions may take on a variety of forms, often obscure to students exactly what shape the text should take. Without this knowledge of purposes of arguments, students are left to figure out the type of argument on their own.

In addition to purposes, the C3 Framework Dimension 4 offers multiple formats and technologies in which students can "present adaptations of arguments and explanations on topics of interest to others to reach audiences and venues outside the classroom using print and oral technologies (e.g.,

Table 3.1 Types and Purposes of Arguments

Type of argument	Purpose of argument	Examples	Formats
Interpretation (one-sided argument)	Argue for a particular interpretation without necessarily recognizing alternative perspectives.	Should the right to vote be protected by the Constitution?	Poster Letter Blog Map
Critique	Argue against a particular interpretation made by someone else. Similar to an interpretation or "one-sided argument," critiques also require students to share claims, evidence, and reasoning. However, in critiques, students' claims express what they reject or question in another person's argument.	Does money matter in political campaigns?	Essay Digital documentary Debate Speech Social media post Billboard Meme Powerpoint Speech Infographics
Counter-argument	Present a counterargument that recognizes and rebuts interpretations or evidence that challenge their position sharing challenging or conflicting claims and evidence.		
Discussion (both sides of an issue)	To discuss two or more sides of an issue.	Pros and cons of the electoral college	

Sources: Adapted from Read.Inquire.Write. and Derewianka and Jones (2016).

posters, essays, letters, debates, speeches, reports, and maps) and digital technologies (e.g., Internet, social media, and digital documentary)" (p. 60).

As we alluded to above, it is important not to confuse genre with format or technology (column 4 Formats in Table 3.1). One way these get confused is when formats are equated to genres. Another way students can get confused is when we call writing products "essays." In the vignette, the teacher told students to write an *essay* about the electoral college. The word "essay" is problematic in itself. An essay can be a one-sided argument without seeking alternative views; for example, state why electoral college works for the United States. An essay can also be a critique, where a student critiques a widely held interpretation by rejecting or questioning other people's central argument that the electoral college is an effective process by which people choose their president. An essay can also be a two-sided argument where students rebut interpretations or evidence by presenting counterclaims (Read. Inquire. Write). "Essay" is not a genre. It is a format that can take any shape of text depending on the social purpose of the genre.

> Look back at the vignette that starts this chapter. What type of argument is Ms. Beatty looking for? Rewrite the assignment so that the genre and type of explanation are more clear.

We are thinking that Ms. Beatty is looking for a discussion argument. The purpose of this type of argument is to present an issue from two or more perspectives, giving each side equal weight or sometimes favoring one side depending on the weight of the evidence. When students write or orally present discussion arguments, they are expected to adjust intensity of their argument, recognize strengths and weaknesses in others' arguments, express both positive and negative attitudes, and be mindful of how the audience can be positioned by the writer (Derewianka & Jones, 2023). A discussion primarily includes a statement of the issue and then a consideration of different sides of the argument before a summarizing recommendation. Ms. Beatty could give students a model response or mentor text like the one below which would show students what she expects them to produce (See below). We discuss how to efficiently create mentor texts like this in Chapter 4. Note, this is an excerpt from a complete text in the Appendix.

As you read, the writer here chose to give both sides equal weight and presented a fairly balanced perspective on each perspective. The writer chose to structure their argument as follows:

- Issue and background:
  - Preview of each perspective
- Position A (pros):
  - Points 1–3
  - Evidence or example for each point
- Position B (cons):
  - Points 1–4
  - Evidence or example for each point
- Summary of each side

Mentor Text with Pros and Cons of the U.S. Electoral College System

Pros and Cons of the U.S. Electoral College System

Most people don't know that in the United States the person with the most votes doesn't win the presidency. There have been many times when the person with the most votes lost being president. This is called the popular vote, but the person who wins the popular vote doesn't win. The person who wins the electoral college vote wins. The electoral college is an alternative to electing the president by popular vote. In this process, the states elect the President and Vice President.

So what is the difference? There are pros and cons to the electoral college, and some people say we should eliminate it and only use the popular vote to decide who wins the presidency. Here are reasons why the electoral college is good, and reasons why it is bad. You can decide for yourself.

Why the Electoral College is Good – Pros

1. It Keeps Smaller States Relevant in National Politics
   In a U.S. presidential election, if we had no electoral college, then only the popular vote would matter. Then candidates might concentrate their energies on densely populated metro areas like New York, Los Angeles, and Chicago because that is where most of the votes would be. Depending on your perspective, that might sound like a change for the worse. It would mean candidates would have little reason to consider going to Nebraska or Kansas.

   ....

2. When the electoral college completes its vote, that means the election is finished
   The electoral college makes U.S. presidential elections less undecided by providing a clear ending. There's no need for a national recount when you have an electoral college.

   ....

Arguments

> ### *Why the Electoral College is Bad – Cons*
>
> 1. People Feel Like Their Vote Doesn't Matter
>   There is an old saying that "every vote counts," which is very true, **but** if you vote for a candidate that doesn't win due to the electoral votes, then you might feel like your vote doesn't count. In the electoral college, it's true that not every vote matters. Some states will swing Democrat or Republican even if you don't vote, so you might think your vote doesn't count. Some people think that eliminating the electoral college would be an easy way to raise the number of people who vote because they will think that their vote counts more. This will boost Americans' engagement in the political process.
> 2. It Gives Too Much Power to Swing States
>   If you follow U.S. federal elections and see that the news channels focus on those states that could go either way, Democrat or Republican, you might find yourself in a state in which this decision has already been made....

The structure above is different from Figure 3.1 because it adds a more nuanced way of naming the stages in the argument genre. Introduction, Body, Conclusion are not specific enough and often, students struggle with their organization because one can write any genre with Introduction, Body, Conclusion. In this chapter, we take up a more nuanced way of naming the stages specific to different kinds of arguments.

Once we have established what type of argument we want our students to write, the next thing we need to do is think about the generic structure of that argument. At face value, the generic structure looks like an outline, but we need to go further and think about the function of each section of that outline. As we saw above, it is not enough to say write an introduction and then list pros and cons and add a conclusion. Students need to know the function or job of the introduction in a discussion argument because the jobs are specific to the type of argument. In other words, we need to take a close look at disciplinary reasoning we are expecting and how this relates to the content in each section of the discussion argument.

Consider Table 3.2 that fleshes out both the jobs and the content, chunking the discussion argument into four distinct stages.

We have found it helpful to provide students with the left side of a table like this that includes naming the genre stages and identifying their jobs. What this does is build student awareness of writing each section to carry out a specific purpose. For example, for the first stage students need

Arguments

Table 3.2 Discussion Argument Genre Stages

Discussion argument genre structure	Jot down your ideas for content for each section
I. Issue and background: • Preview of each perspective **Job of this stage:** State the issue, provide brief background on the issue, previous each perspective	• Popular vote • Electoral college process • Pros and cons previewed

II. Position A (pros):
• Points 1–3
• Elaboration, evidence, or example for each point
Job of this stage: State each pro-electoral college each side and provide either elaboration or evidence with examples when necessary
	• Pro #1:
	  • Small states are relevant (NY or CA don't hold all the voting power)
	  • Elaboration
	• Pro #2:
	  • Provides a clear ending (no recount necessary)
	  • Elaboration
	• Pro #3:
	  • Makes campaigning easier
	  • Elaboration

III. Position B (cons):
• Points 1–4
• Evidence or example for each point
Job of this stage: State each con (against) electoral college each side and provide either elaboration or evidence with examples when necessary
	• Con #1:
	  • People feel their vote doesn't matter
	  • Elaboration
	• Con #2:
	  • Swing states get too much power
	  • Elaboration
	• Con #3:
	  • Can clash with the popular vote
	  • Elaboration
	• Con #4:
	  • The possibility of "Rogue Electors"
	  • Elaboration

IV. Summary **Job of this stage:** Provide high level summary	• Review city versus country people perspectives

to consider, what are the important pieces of information they would need to include to provide background on an issue? Then, for the second stage, they would need to think about how they would preview the pros and cons? What details should they include that they can expand upon? Once students understand what they are aiming to do in a section, or the job of the section, then they can think about how to do that job with content.

Note, in this chapter, we focus on discussion arguments (two-sided arguments). As you move on to other types of arguments, consult Table 3.1 to help you think of other types of arguments in social studies and what generic organizational structures you would use to teach students how to organize other types of arguments. As you have seen in the example above, there is more nuance in our approach to the organization than just claim, evidence, and reasoning.

Teaching students how to plan their writing using genre stages and jobs for each stage will go a long way in improving students' writing. However, if we stop our writing instruction at this point, we have answered the *what* part of writing, but we still haven't addressed the *how* part of writing. For example, *how* do we use language to "provide a balanced perspective on an issue" in a pro/con argument? How do we use language to express our content? What kinds of language features do we choose amongst? In the next section, we delve into the *how* by focusing on the language writers use when moderating intensity in arguments to avoid polarization.

Part 3: Language Features in Social Studies Discussion Arguments. What Language Do We Need to Moderate Our Position? How Do We Use Language to Moderate the Intensity of Arguments?

In the previous section, we looked at arguments at the genre level, studying the text-level characteristics and thinking about the different purposes of arguments, which are primarily to state claims and provide evidentiary reasoning. However, as we have argued, looking at the organizational features of text at the genre level is not enough to teach the language of argumentation. We also need to attend to the language features present in

Table 3.3 Language Features Common to Arguments

Possible language features

Discourse (Text and Paragraphs) Dimension:

- Text connectors to signal alternate points of view (on the other hand, contrary to common belief, according to); show concession or comparison/contrast (while, although)
- A variety of clauses to frame details, examples, quotes, data (according to, historians dis/agree, several sources suggest)

Sentence Dimension:

- Complex sentences to create concession (e.g., *While … Despite … Although …*)
- Compound sentences to elaborate one's reasoning (e.g., *So if you live in the city, you probably think that the electoral college is bad, but if you live in rural areas, you would probably like the way we elect our president as it is*)
- Simple sentences to state the point clearly (e.g., *The electoral college provides a clear and decisive result in the presidential election*)

Word (and Word Group) Dimension:

- Modality resources (verbs, nouns, adjectives, and phrases) to open spaces for other possibilities (e.g., *it **might be** of benefit to smaller states*)
- Phrases to align with the audience (*you may have heard, of course, we all know that …*)
- Generalized nouns to represent key concepts (e.g., *voting, politics*)
- Expanded noun groups (e.g., *American presidential elections*)
- Reporting verbs to quote and report from sources (*claim, suggest, contradict, conclude*)
- Evaluative verbs, adverbs, and adjectives to add author's perspective (*dominated, absolutely, compelling*)

Sources: Adapted from Brisk (2023) and Derewianka and Jones (2023).

arguments. What follows is a list of language features that typically occur in social studies arguments (Table 3.3).

In Chapter 2, at the register level, we looked at the language features of explanations such as text connectives, expanded noun groups, and cohesion. We also looked at how those features expressed two metafunctions: Field and Mode. Those metafunctions and features are also relevant to the argument genre. And if you want to teach those features when teaching arguments, feel free to use those exercises and tables to teach cohesion,

Arguments

expanded noun group, and text connectives because they also exist in arguments. We are going to add to your repertoire of language features by focusing on Tenor, and the modality resources in particular as these are very important in arguments. Tenor is concerned with the interactions and relationships we establish with the reader or listener. Tenor resources, illustrated in Table 3.4, are critical for arguments. Here's why.

Imagine you read a text like this:

> People don't know that in the United States the person with the most votes doesn't win the presidency. When the person got the most votes, they lost being president. This is called the popular vote, but the person who wins the popular vote doesn't win. The person who wins the electoral college vote wins. The electoral college is an alternative to electing the president by popular vote. In this process, the States elect the President and Vice President.
>
> So what is the difference? There are pros and cons to the electoral college, and everyone says we must eliminate it and only use the popular vote to decide who wins the presidency. Here are reasons why the electoral college is good, and reasons why it is bad. You must decide for yourself.

The content of that paragraph is solid. The writer structured the text well and the ideas flow. The writer even knew how to create cohesion from sentence to sentence to add clarity to the ideas. But there is something a little bit off in that text. In some instances, you may have noticed that the writer comes off "too strong." They used language like "you must" and "we must." In addition, if you look more closely, you'll notice word choices like "everyone" and "people" send a message that all means all, and everyone agrees. When claims are made without tempering or moderation, Derewianka (2023) calls them "bare assertions." To illustrate bare assertions, let's use an example: "The Electoral college is not a flawed system." In it, there is "no ambiguity, no multiple meanings, not attempt to entertain alternatives" (Derewianka, 2023, p. 111). Derewianka says that "if we simply make bare assertions, there is little sensitivity to other possibilities and perspectives and interaction tends to be restricted to the level of either agreeing or disagreeing" (p. 111). It is important that our students

Table 3.4 Language Resources for Interacting with the Reader or Listener

Functions	Grammatical resources (or language features)	Examples
Open spaces to other possibilities through modality	Modal verbs Modal nouns Modal adverbs Modal adjectives (elaborated in Table 3.5) **Sensing verbs** Think, believe, bet, guess	• **Might** concentrate their energies … • That **might sound** like a change … • It **would mean** candidates would have • Democrats **may think** … • Some analysts **think** … • They **believe** … • I guess
Bring in other voices, and introduce other perspectives	Attribution or reference to other individuals, statistics, research	Vague references: • Some analysts suggest … • Most people agree that … • Politicians **say** … Specific references: • According to the U.S. Constitution, Article II, Section 1 … • Johnson and Vaughn (1987) claim that …
Countering or challenging an idea	Text connectives	• While … • Although …
To build alliance with the reader/listener	Use of personal pronoun "you" Phrases *as you can imagine, we all know*	• **You** can decide for yourself • If **you** follow U.S. federal elections … • **You** are actually voting for electors … • So if **you** live in the city, you probably think
Adjust the strength and focus on one's attitude or perspective	Graduation resources such as: • adverbs *absolutely, extremely, utterly, very, truly, somewhat, most, simply, never*	• A **truly** national coalition • Aren't **necessarily** the most representative of the country as a whole • **Most** people think …

(Continued)

Arguments

Table 3.4 (Continued)

Functions	Grammatical resources (or language features)	Examples
Engage the reader and capture their attention	Use of questions	• So what is the difference? • So which is better, the popular vote or the electoral vote?
Other resources for interacting with readers	• Noun groups: *Upheaval, national cohesion* • Evaluative adjectives: *Stable, peaceful, rogue, faithless* • Qualifiers: *Some, most, one* reason, *the main* reason	• "Rogue" or "faithless" electors • You can just do a recount in that state rather than creating national **upheaval**

know how to create a more neutral stance when writing arguments. Students tend to use overly emotional language in their arguments or to present their claims as undeniable truths and bare assertions (Derewianka & Jones (2023). What most students need to learn as they expand their linguistic repertoires and be taken seriously as argument writers, is how to distance themselves from the issue by using less emotional language by tempering their position. This does not mean that students should not be passionate about their issues; instead, they should remain passionate but use less emotionally charged language to communicate their ideas.

What we are talking about here, about stating claims as undeniable truths, or tempering them, is how we enact the interpersonal metafunction, tenor. Basically, every time we speak, write, or communicate in any way through words, pictures, sound, or gestures, we enact a relationship with our audience. That's why it's called interpersonal because it is not about what we say, but it's how we say it. We communicate what we value through our words. Let's take a look at this quote.

> "Under systemic functional perspectives, ... there is no utterance that is without interpersonal value. Nevertheless, the influence of the common-sense notion of the 'fact' is widespread and it may be tempting to see some utterances as more interpersonal than others.

> Under the heteroglossic orientation, however, we are reminded that even the most 'factual' utterances ... are nevertheless interpersonally charged in that they enter into relationships of tension with a related set of alternative and contradictory utterances. The degree of that tension is socially determined."

That quote includes terminology like heteroglossic (which means "different voices" hetero+glossic) but it basically says that every time we communicate, we communicate with other audiences, close or distant, and we insert our values and perspectives into what we say. Even opinions can be presented as facts, and facts can be presented as opinions, just look at the same sentence "The electoral college is not a flawed system." It is someone's opinion and it is presented as fact.

Now, that we explained what we mean by interpersonal language resources and their power, let's come back to our text and the words like "you must" and "we must," "everyone" and "always." We are not saying here that those are **always** wrong choices. We are saying that it all depends on the social purpose and how you want to position yourself in relation to the issue you communicate. Do you want to distance yourself or get all emotional about it? There are times for all of those choices. In this chapter, we are going to talk about a range of choices we can make related to tenor in writing arguments, so that we can teach those choices to our students so they can make informed choices in academic and personal writing. Interpersonal language resources are important every time we communicate, not only in school assignments.

Table 3.5 provides a list of key language features necessary for opening spaces for other possibilities, establishing a perspective, creating a relationship with a reader, avoid polarization, acknowledge and rebut alternate positions, and many others.

There are many functions and language features in the table above that you can use when teaching arguments. We are going to focus on two functions: (1) Open spaces for other possibilities through modality and (2) bring in other voices into our writing through modality and bring in other voices, and introduce other perspectives through attribution.

Arguments

Open Spaces for Other Possibilities through Modality

When writing arguments, students need to learn how to state their position firmly but in a way that does not alienate their audience and open spaces for other possibilities. There are many language resources that may help us be inclusive of other possibilities. One such language feature is modality. Derewianka and Jones (2023) describe modality as "the distance between yes and no; it is sometimes that 'wiggle room' and can be expressed in varying degrees from low to high" (p. 246). Modality can be achieved through verbs, nouns, adjectives, and even phrases.

We will go through modality language features in detail and give you exercises to try out and ideas for your classroom. Our goal is to empower you to teach these features to your students. Most students will need your support in making these features visible and in understanding how they work to communicate the social studies content.

Take a look at the excerpt below to see modality in the context of the electoral college text. The highlighted examples show instances of modality.

> If you follow U.S. federal elections and see that the news channels focus on those states that could go either way, Democrat or Republican, you might find yourself in a state in which this decision has already been made. If you don't live in a swing state, like Pennsylvania, Florida, Ohio, Michigan, Wisconsin, and more, you probably won't see as many ads, have as many canvassers come to your door or get polled as frequently. The electoral college means that swing states – which aren't necessarily the most representative of the country as a whole – get most of the attention.

We can characterize modality as being high, medium, or low. Study the chart in Table 3.5 below.

Take any of the language features from Table 3.5 and write your own sentences in the table below.

High	Medium	Low

Arguments

Table 3.5 High, Medium, Low Modality Chart

Language feature	High	Medium	Low
Modal Verbs	Must, need, has to	Will, would, supposed to	Can, may, might
Sensing Verbs	Know, believe	Think	Guess, suppose
Adverbs	Certainly, definitely, absolutely, undoubtedly	Probably, usually, likely, apparently, presumably	Possibly, perhaps, maybe, likely, supposedly
Adjectives	Certain, definite, absolute	Probable, usual	Possible, potential
Nouns	Certainty, necessity, requirement, obligation	Probability	Possibility
Clauses and Phrases	I believe that … I know that … Everyone knows that There is absolutely no doubt Without any hesitation	In my opinion	According to …

Sources: Based on Brisk (2023) and Derewianka and Jones (2023).

Now let's take a look at our electoral college mentor text and consider how modality can go from low to high (Table 3.6).

Now using the table below, fill in the blanks and discuss the change in meaning from low to medium to high modality. Take some time to reflect on your own uses of modality in your own writing and speaking. You will most likely have fun with it, like we do. Let's be modality nerds together!

Possibly, perhaps, maybe, arguably	Probably, presumably, apparently	Definitely, absolutely, certainly, surely, undoubtedly
but if you live in rural areas, you _____ like the way we elect our president as it is.	but if you live in rural areas, you _____ like the way we elect our president as it is.	but if you live in rural areas, you _____ like the way we elect our president as it is.

77

Arguments

Table 3.6 Examples of Modality with Sentences from the Mentor Text

Low →	Medium →	High
May, might, could, would	Will, should, can, need to	Must, shall, ought to, has to
This might boost Americans' engagement in the political process.	This will boost Americans' engagement in the political process.	This has to boost Americans' engagement in the political process.
You could decide for yourself.	You should decide for yourself.	You must decide for yourself
Possibly, perhaps, maybe, arguably	Probably, presumably, apparently	Definitely, absolutely, certainly, surely, undoubtedly
So if you live in the city, you perhaps think that the electoral college is bad …	So if you live in the city, you probably think that the electoral college is bad …	So if you live in the city, you absolutely think that the electoral college is bad …

Now write your own sentence here.

Possibly, perhaps, maybe, arguably	Probably, presumably, apparently	Definitely, absolutely, certainly, surely, undoubtedly

Take a look at the excerpt of our text below, and highlight the examples of modality and then characterize them as high, medium, or low. The modality is highlighted for you. Your job is to identify whether it's high, medium, or low.

There is an old saying that "every vote counts," which is very true, **but** if you vote for a candidate that doesn't win due to the electoral votes, then you might feel like your vote doesn't count. In the electoral college, it's true that not every vote matters. Some states will swing Democrat or Republican even if you don't vote, so you might think your vote doesn't count. Some people think that eliminating the

Arguments

> electoral college would be an easy way to raise the number of people who vote because they will think that their vote counts more. This will boost Americans' engagement in the political process.

Other means through which intensity of argument is achieved are through words like *somewhat, some, utterly, allegedly, extremely, urgently,* and others. In our mentor text above, there were several examples where instead of claiming that *all people* or *everyone* thinks this, the author moderated it with words like *some* or *many*.

Let's take a look at one sentence from our text (Table 3.7). The original is on the left with the modality (moderation) resources highlighted. They leave room for other possibilities. The contrast is on the right where "some" is replaced with "everyone" and "could make" is replaced with "will make" closing doors for other possibilities. Most teachers call this "hedging." You can definitely continue using that word. All we are adding is the range of resources hedging can be done with. You can use this exercise to show students the different meanings and discuss which one opens the door for other perspectives and why. Draw your students' attention that the written example with the stronger modality is not necessarily better and invite students to reflect on their language choices and notice their own tendencies in language and how our own language can open or close doors for other possibilities.

In the rewritten column in Table 3.7, we replaced "some" with everyone and the verb "say" with "argues." We are going to elaborate on the reporting verbs later in this chapter.

Now try this on your own and then with your students in your classroom (the below table). Rewrite the statement on the left with a weaker modality. Please note the seemingly invisible verb "is" actually plays a critical role in creating stronger modality. It can be replaced with "sounds like," "could be," or other verb group options from Table 3.5.

Table 3.7 Contrast of Modality

Original (weaker modality)	Rewritten (stronger modality)
Some say that getting rid of the electoral college could make American presidential elections even more expensive than they already are.	Everyone argues that getting rid of the electoral college will make American presidential elections even more expensive than they already are.

Arguments

3.1 Try it out

3.1 Stronger modality	Weaker modality
That **is** a change for the worse. It **means** candidates **have no reason** to consider going to Nebraska or Kansas.	

In the following table, try revising the sentence to make the modality stronger.

3.2 Try it out

3.2 Stronger modality	Weaker modality
	Some argue that eliminating the electoral college **might** increase voter engagement, as people **could** perceive their votes as more influential.

And in following table, try going from weaker modality to stronger:

3.3 Try it out

3.3 Weaker modality	Stronger modality
Eliminating the electoral college could ensure that the popular vote determines the outcome of the election.	

In the example above, skipping the modal verbs altogether intensifies the argument and closes doors for other possibilities. You could discuss with your students the change of meaning in both as well as when it would be appropriate to use weaker and stronger modalities.

If your students need further support, try focusing on modality in everyday conversations, not related to the electoral college topic. For example, they can use the examples below. Have them act out or discuss **how language opens and closes spaces for other possibilities.**

Table 3.8 Language of Absolutes versus Language of Moderation

Language of absolutes	Language of moderation
He **is** the best candidate to represent his party.	He **seems to be** a good candidate to represent his party. **Some voters say** he is the best candidate to represent his party.
This system discourages voter turnout.	**Some argue** that this system can discourage voter turnout.

That's a possible way to go about it.	That's the only way to go about it.	This could be a way to go about it.

Write out sentences below to have low, medium, and high modalities. Follow the example.

You are wrong.	You could be wrong.	You are absolutely wrong.

Discuss with students how we may need to use modality to avoid speaking in the language of absolutes when it's not necessary. Sometimes, it's important to state our claims in absolutes; however, we also need to learn how to moderate our stance. Look at the examples above (Table 3.8).

Bring in Other Voices, and Introduce Other Perspectives through Attribution

In Table 3.4, we saw that to engage with the other voices or introduce other perspectives, we need to attribute other ideas or refer to other individuals, statistics, and research. That's called attribution. Below is the excerpt from Table 3.4.

Engage with other voices, introduce other perspectives, and bring in evidence	Attribution or reference to other individuals, statistics, research	Vague references: • Some analysts **suggest** … • Most people **agree** that … • Politicians **say** … Specific references: • According to the U.S. Constitution, Article II, Section 1 … • Johnson and Vaughn (1987) claim that …

Arguments

Table 3.9 Vague v. Specific Attribution

Vague Attribution:
- Some believe/believe/argue/disagree …
- Some people say …
- There is a widely held belief is …
- Many sources claim that …
- According to …
- It is commonly known that …

Specific Attribution:
- According to the U.S. Constitution, Article II, Section 1 …
- Johnson and Vaughn (1987) claim that …

Let's take a look at the examples of attribution in Tables 3.9 and 3.10. Note that when we say attribution, we don't just mean "cite your sources." It's actually more nuanced than that. For example, we might choose to say "some argue that" because we want to attribute that claim to others; otherwise, it will sound like it was just our own opinion. The source, of course, is also added at the end of that claim, as shown here. Other language resources for attrition are "according to" etc.

Now, try to identify attribution to this sentence.

3.4 Try it out

According to an article published by the National Conference of State Legislatures (NCSL) in 2021, the electoral college consists of 538 electors who cast votes to select the President and Vice President.

Attribution is mostly done through verbs and as we have discussed modality above, some verbs are weaker and some carry stronger modality. For example, verbs like *comment, discuss, note, state, acknowledge* carry a more neutral meaning. And verbs like *critique, accuse, complain* have a stronger meaning (Table 3.12).

Derewianka (2023) lists a practical application of attribution to providing feedback on student work. We have selected a few key questions you may use with your students. See Table 3.11.

Table 3.10 Example: No attribution v. Vague Attribution

This system can discourage voter turnout, particularly in states where the outcome is already predicted.

Some argue that this system can discourage voter turnout, particularly in states where the outcome is already predicted (Brookings Institution – "The Electoral College and the Myth of a Single American National Election Day").

To describe these verbs used in attribution, we can use the term "reporting verbs" and instead of just verbs because there are many different kinds of verbs that we use in writing, but when we bring in other voices and cite our sources, we use a special kind of verb, "reporting verbs." Have a look at Table 3.12 and one activity you can do with students is to have them cut up these reporting verbs and have them group by the weaker, neutral, and stronger position before they use them in their own writing. We have also placed this table in the Appendix for you to use as a resource for this task.

Why such focus on modality? Because it is a major resource for how writers or speakers position themselves in relation to the issue and the audience to whom they deliver their message. We definitely don't want you to work on the modal nouns or verbs or adverbs without any attention to the function. This is not about identifying parts of speech. This is about teaching students how to be informed choice makers when they write arguments. For extra practice with these get stronger at the interpersonal language resources, such as modality, you could go back to the whole mentor text in the Appendix and identify all the instances where you recognize that the writer enacted a particular relationship and

Table 3.11 Questions to ask students to teach attribution

- Has the writer considered other positions or sources of information? Or is the text "single-voiced," relying solely on the insights of the writer?
- How are vague references to other voices (e.g., Researchers have found that …; Is often said that …, In the literature …)?
- Have "opposing camps" been recognized in terms of their spokespersons (e.g., In contrast to Halliday, Chomsky argues that …)?
- What degree of commitment has been indicated through the use of reporting verbs such as suggest, claim, insist?

(Derewiaka, 2023, pp. 112–113)

Arguments

Table 3.12 Weaker, Neutral, and Stronger Position Reporting Verbs by Their Function

Function/Position	Weaker position	Neutral position	Stronger position
agreement	admits, concedes	accepts, acknowledges, agrees, concurs, confirms, recognizes	praises, supports
argument and persuasion	apologizes	assures, encourages, interprets, justifies, reasons	alerts, argues, contends, convinces, emphasizes, forbids, insists, proves, promises, persuades, threatens, warns
believing	guesses, hopes, imagines	believes, claims, declares, expresses, feels, holds, knows, maintains, professes, subscribes to, thinks	asserts, guarantees, insists, upholds
conclusion		concludes, discovers, finds, infers, realizes	
disagreement and questioning	doubts, questions	challenges, debates, disagrees, questions, requests, wonders	accuses, attacks, complains, contradicts, criticizes, denies, discards, disclaims, discounts, dismisses, disputes, disregards, negates, objects to, opposes, refutes, rejects

(Continued)

Table 3.12 (Continued)

Function/Position	Weaker position	Neutral position	Stronger position
evaluation and examination		analyses, appraises, assesses, compares, considers, contrasts, critiques, evaluates, examines, investigates, understands	blames, complains, ignores, scrutinizes, warns
suggestion	alleges, intimates, speculates	advises, advocates, hypothesizes, posits, postulates, proposes, suggests, theorizes	asserts, recommends, urges

Sources: Excerpted from University of Adelaide Writing Center.

positioned themselves in a particular way toward the issue of the electoral college. When you are ready to check your work, you'll find the answers in the Appendix. You may wish to have your students use Table 3.13 below, which focuses on just two paragraphs. It can be overwhelming for students to work with a whole text when they are just learning to identify a key language feature.

Table 3.13 Instances of Modality in Our Mentor Text

Excerpt from Our Mentor Text Pros and Cons of the U.S. Electoral College System
Most people don't know that in the United States the person with the most votes doesn't win the presidency. There have been many times when the person with the most votes lost being president. This is called the popular vote, but the person who wins the popular vote doesn't win. The person who wins the electoral college vote wins. The electoral college is an alternative to electing the president by popular vote. In this process, the States elect the President and Vice President.
So what is the difference? There are pros and cons to the electoral college, and some people say we should eliminate it and only use the popular vote to decide who wins the presidency. Here are reasons why the electoral college is good, and reasons why it is bad. You can decide for yourself.

Arguments

Summary

This chapter provided an overview of different kinds of arguments in social studies, their organizational and key language features, focusing on language for avoiding polarization and how to open spaces for other possibilities with our language choices. All of those language choices enact the relationship with the reader or listener and constitute a major part of the interpersonal metafunction, or tenor, in our language system.

At the sentence and word level, this chapter focused on modality. It is important to teach students how to moderate their stance because it helps avoid single-voiced statements, especially when students are learning how to lead productive conversations. When our students realize the power of their language and, in particular, how language can open or shut down conversations and dialog, they can engage in democracy building in more productive ways.

Now if Ms. Beatty was equipped with all the information about from this chapter, how might she have taught the lesson differently?

Vignette: Reprisal

T: We've been talking a lot about the electoral college, you've done the research, reviewed multiple sources for both sides, and it's time to write an essay.

S: Essay, essay, essay, not another essay!

T: You're gonna thank me later. Writing will help you really clarify what you think you know.

S1: Yeah, we know that you don't win the presidency by a popular vote. Remember what happened to Hillary in 2016? She won by 2.3 million votes! This whole electoral college is so unfair. My mother is still mad about it.

S2: It **may seem unfair** but imagine if we had to do a recount! Let's count up all 200 million ballots just to double check! In the electoral college you just count the elector's votes, I could do that in my math class!

T: Hey, you two are having a great discussion! As you made it clear, there are pros and cons to this system and guess what, you are going to write about both sides. And I particularly appreciated how S2 changed the statement from This is unfair! To "This may seem unfair" to open spaces for other possibilities. As you write your pros and con argument, make sure to present both sides equally, and cite your evidence to include other voices, not just your bare assertions. Let's practice these examples through some exercises. Here's the outline for this week and how we will practice these before you are going to write your own argument (Figure 3.2).

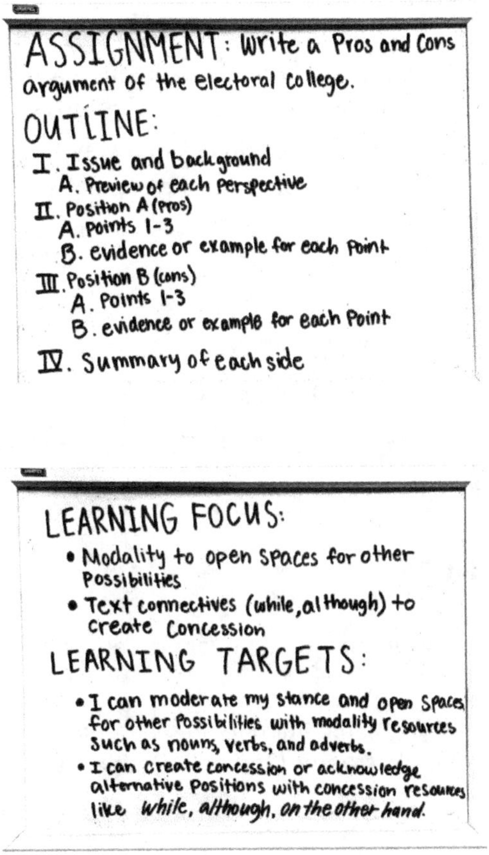

ASSIGNMENT: Write a Pros and Cons argument of the electoral college.

OUTLINE:
I. Issue and background
    A. Preview of each perspective
II. Position A (Pros)
    A. Points 1-3
    B. evidence or example for each point
III. Position B (cons)
    A. Points 1-3
    B. evidence or example for each point
IV. Summary of each side

LEARNING FOCUS:
- Modality to open spaces for other possibilities
- Text connectives (while, although) to create concession

LEARNING TARGETS:
- I can moderate my stance and open spaces for other possibilities with modality resources such as nouns, verbs, and adverbs.
- I can create concession or acknowledge alternative positions with concession resources like while, although, on the other hand.

Figure 3.2 Ms. Beatty (after)

Arguments

On the Board

Low	Medium	High
May, might, could, would	Will, should, can, need to	Must, shall, ought to, has to
This might boost Americans' engagement in the political process.	This can boost Americans' engagement in the political process.	This will boost Americans' engagement in the political process.

Task: Discuss each sentence in terms of which statement opens spaces for other possibilities and which one closes.

In this revised vignette, we see that Ms. Beatty didn't just assign writing and gave students a generic outline but taught a specific outline for the pros and cons argument. In addition, she included a language focus and an explicit focus on learning targets that focused on the key language resources needed for writing an argument in a way that opens spaces for other possibilities and acknowledges other perspectives.

Notes

1. https://c3teachers.org/inquiries/
2. https://c3teachers.org/inquiries/electoral-college/
3. https://c3teachers.org/inquiries/democracy-in-danger-voting-rights/
4. https://c3teachers.org/inquiries/campaign-finance/

References

Appraisal https://www.grammatics.com/appraisal/appraisaloutline/framed/frame.htm

Brisk, M. E. (2023). *Engaging students in academic literacies: SFL genre pedagogy for K-8 classrooms* (2nd ed.). Routledge.

Coffin, C. (2009). *Historical discourse. The language of time, cause and evaluation*. Bloomsbury.

College, Career, and Civics Framework for States' Social Studies Standards. National Council for Social Studies Standards.

Derewianka, B. (2023). *A new grammar companion for teachers*. PETAA.

Derewianka, B., & Jones, P. (2023). *Teaching language in context* (3rd ed.). Oxford University Press.

de Oliveira, L. C., & Obenchain, K. (2019). *Teaching history and social studies to English language learners: Preparing pre-service and in-service teachers*. Palgrave MacMillan.

Read.Inquire.Write Argument Writing Progression https://readinquirewrite.umich.edu/writing-progression/

Schleppegrell, M. (2004). *The language of schooling. A functional linguistics perspective*. Laurence Earlbaum Publishers.

Verbs for Reporting. Writing Center Learning Guide. University of Adelaide. https://www.adelaide.edu.au/writingcentre/sites/default/files/docs/learningguide-verbsforreporting.pdf

Chapter 3 Appendix

COMPLETE MENTOR TEXT (with modality highlighted): Pros and Cons of the U.S. Electoral College System

Most people don't know that in the United States the person with the most votes doesn't win the presidency. There have been many times when the person with the most votes lost being president. This is called the popular vote, but the person who wins the popular vote doesn't win. The person who wins the electoral college vote wins. The electoral college is an alternative to electing the president by popular vote. In this process, the States elect the President and Vice President.

So what is the difference? There are pros and cons to the electoral college, and some people say we should eliminate it and only use the popular vote to decide who wins the presidency. Here are reasons why the electoral college is good, and reasons why it is bad. You can decide for yourself.

Why the Electoral College is Good – Pros

1. It Keeps Smaller States Relevant in National Politics
   In a U.S. presidential election, if we had no electoral college, then only the popular vote would matter. Then candidates might concentrate

Arguments

their energies on densely populated metro areas like New York, Los Angeles, and Chicago because that is where most of the votes would be. Depending on your perspective, that might sound like a change for the worse. It would mean candidates would have little reason to consider going to Nebraska or Kansas.

One reason that some analysts support the electoral college is that it encourages candidates to pay attention to small states and not just get out the vote in big, populous states and cities. The electoral college gives small states more weight in the political process than their population would otherwise confer. This is the main reason for having an electoral college rather than just a popular vote.

2. When the electoral college completes its vote, that means the election is finished

   The electoral college makes U.S. presidential elections less undecided by providing a clear ending. There's no need for a national recount when you have an electoral college.

   If one state has voting issues, you can just do a recount in that state rather than creating national upheaval. That means whoever wins the presidency must build a truly national coalition. This, in turn, helps promote national cohesion and the peaceful transfer of power between presidents and helps keep the nation's political system stable.

3. It Makes it Easier for Candidates to Campaign

   Even though the electoral college makes it more important for candidates to visit the heartland, they can still work on particular states where they think they can win. Democrats may think they can't win in Nebraska, so they can choose not to campaign there. Same for Republicans, who can skip New York or California.

   The fact that certain states and their electoral votes are safely in the column of one party or the other makes it easier and cheaper for candidates to campaign successfully. They can focus their energies on the battleground states. Some argue that getting rid of the electoral college could make American presidential elections even more expensive than they already are. This would mean that the problem with candidate financing could be even worse.

Why the Electoral College is Bad – Cons

1. People Feel Like Their Vote Doesn't Matter
   There is an old saying that "every vote counts," which is very true, **but** if you vote for a candidate that doesn't win due to the electoral votes, then you might feel like your vote doesn't count. In the electoral college, it's true that not every vote matters. Some states will swing Democrat or Republican even if you don't vote, so you might think your vote doesn't count. Some people think that eliminating the electoral college would be an easy way to raise the number of people who vote because they will think that their vote counts more. This will boost Americans' engagement in the political process.

2. It Gives Too Much Power to Swing States
   If you follow U.S. federal elections and see that the news channels focus on those states that could go either way, Democrat or Republican, you might find yourself in a state in which this decision has already been made. If you don't live in a swing state, like Pennsylvania, Florida, Ohio, Michigan, Wisconsin, and more, you probably won't see as many ads, have as many canvassers come to your door or get polled as frequently. The electoral college means that swing states – which aren't necessarily the most representative of the country as a whole – get most of the attention.

3. It Can Clash with the Popular Vote
   Back in 2000, Al Gore won the popular vote in the presidential election, but lost the electoral college, and therefore the presidency. That was enough to turn some Americans off from the electoral college forever. If the U.S. eliminates the electoral college, that scenario would never happen again. The potential for the electoral college to conflict with the result of the popular vote is one of the most commonly cited arguments against the electoral college.

4. There Remains the Possibility of "Rogue Electors"
   Many states have no law requiring electors to vote the way their state has voted. Electors in these states are "unbound." They are referred to as a "rogue" or "faithless" electors, and are free to vote for whoever they want. When voting for president, in a way you are actually voting for electors, people selected by a political party, who then go on in January after the elections and cast their

Arguments

votes, but they are really free to vote for whoever they want to, but this rarely happens.

So which is better, the popular vote or the electoral vote? The electoral college was first created so that people living in the cities didn't have so much power in deciding who was president and give more voice to the rest of the country. So if you live in the city, you probably think that the electoral college is bad, but if you live in rural areas, you would probably like the way we elect our president as it is.

Chapter 3 Answer Key

3.1 Original (stronger modality)	Rewritten (weaker modality)
That sounds like a change for the worse. It means candidates have no reason to consider going to Nebraska or Kansas.	Depending on your perspective, that might sound like a change for the worse. It would mean candidates would have little reason to consider going to Nebraska or Kansas.

3.2 Stronger modality	Weaker modality
Some argue that eliminating the electoral college would increase voter engagement, as people would perceive their votes as more influential.	Some argue that eliminating the electoral college might increase voter engagement, as people could perceive their votes as more influential.

3.3 Weaker modality	Stronger modality
Eliminating the electoral college could ensure that the popular vote determines the outcome of the election.	Eliminating the electoral college would definitely ensure that the popular vote determines the outcome of the election.

3.4

According to an article published by the National Conference of State Legislatures (NCSL) in 2021, the electoral college consists of 538 electors who cast votes to select the President and Vice President.

4 How to Make Language Visible Using the Teaching and Learning Cycle for Disciplinary Genres

This chapter switches focus from *what* needs to be made visible to the practicalities of *how* to make it visible with the purpose of promoting equitable academic achievement. This chapter teaches readers how to design instruction step by step to scaffold the language students need to do the work of explaining through the Teaching and Learning Cycle for Disciplinary Genres (TLC-DG), a pedagogy of apprenticeship into the disciplinary genres. It describes each stage of the TLC-DG and shows how to implement them in the classroom using how to's, scripts, and examples. Included is a description of how to write a mentor text and how to analyze student work for planning and assessment, and how to differentiate for students who have different levels of experience. There is an appendix and answer key at the end of the chapter.

This chapter switches focus from what *needs* to be made visible to the practicalities of *how* to make it visible with the purpose of promoting equitable academic achievement. We will do this by introducing you to a pedagogical framework designed to integrate language, literacy, and content learning called the Teaching Learning Cycle of Disciplinary Genres (TLC-DG). We are use descriptions and checklists to illustrate each stage of the TLC-DG to make language visible and promote equitable academic achievement.

The TLC-DG was originally developed by Joan Rothery and her colleagues in Australia in the 1990s and was simply called The Teaching and Learning Cycle. We have decided to add the DG (Disciplinary Genres)

DOI: 10.4324/9781003302711-4

> **Purpose**
> This chapter is going to help you figure out how to design your instruction step by step to scaffold the language your students need to do the work of explaining through the Teaching and Learning Cycle of Disciplinary Genres (TLC-DG), a pedagogy of apprenticeship into the disciplinary genres. While this chapter uses the explanation genre to illustrate TLC-DG, this process can be applied to any genre such as arguments. In addition, it is going to show you how to integrate language, literacy, and content authentically as students learn social studies.

to be more specific about what we are teaching and learning. In North America, the TLC has been taught and implemented in classrooms by many researchers, practitioners, and our colleagues such as Kathryn Accurso, Maria Brisk, Kelly-Ann Cooney, Luciana de Oliveira, Meg Gebhard, Ruth Harman, and many others. Our adaptation used in this book is shown in Figure 4.1.

This cycle consists of the following stages:

- Planning with the End in Mind
- Building Knowledge of the Field
- Supported Reading
- Modeling/Deconstruction
- Joint Construction
- Independent Writing with support as needed
- Analysis of and Reflection on Student Work

Before we describe each of the stages, it is important to mention at the very beginning that this framework best applies to extended units of study that may span several weeks. You may recognize some activities that you already do in this framework such as building knowledge on the topic, researching the topic, providing experiences, debating an issue, class discussions, and others. You may also notice additional new phases in this framework

Teaching and Learning Cycle for Disciplinary Genres

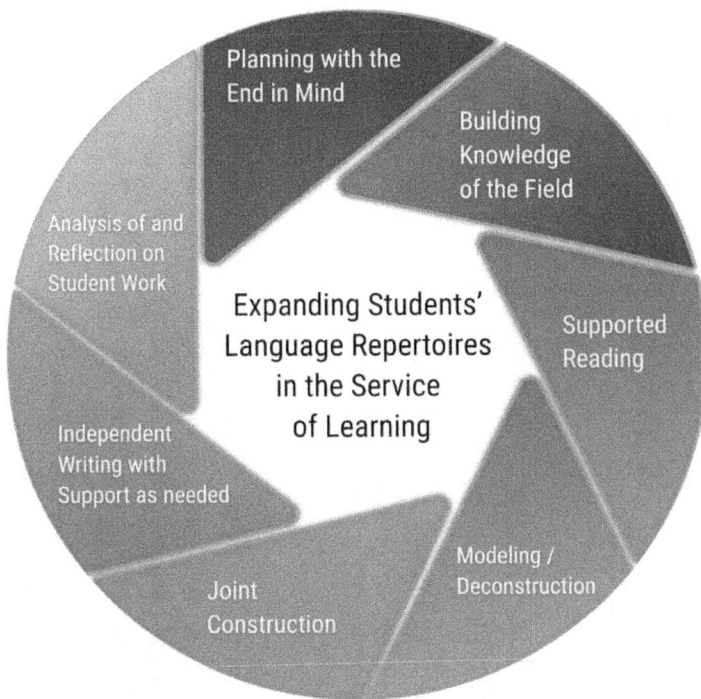

Figure 4.1 The Teaching and Learning Cycle of Disciplinary Genres (TLC-DG)

specifically dedicated to making language visible. We invite you to map your teaching activities onto this framework to integrate and coordinate what you are already doing instead of looking at this framework as "another thing to do." Use Table 4.1 to do a quick self-assessment of what activities you already are doing and which ones you need to focus on to make language more visible. The purpose is to reflect on your instruction where it is strong and where you need to realign your instruction to better support your readers and writers with academic texts. For example, in our research, we found that teachers were good at building the field and knowledge on the topic but needed to do more of the supported reading, deconstruction, joint construction, and analysis of student work in relation to genre. If that is true for you, we invite you to pay close attention to the descriptions of those stages in this chapter and to integrate them into your curriculum units.

We will now describe each of the stages and illustrate them using examples from the previous chapter on explanations.

Teaching and Learning Cycle for Disciplinary Genres

Table 4.1 Teacher Self-Assessment of the Stages of the Teaching and Learning Cycle and the Corresponding Activities

Activities for each stage of the teaching and learning cycle	Self-assessment	
	I do this	*Wondering about*
Planning with the End in Mind		
• Identify standards addressed in the unit.		
• Identify summative assessment that's connected to the central or compelling question in the inquiry.		
• Identify the genre in the summative assessment (e.g., explanations or arguments).		
• Write a mentor text that matches the summative assessment.		
• Do a pretest to assess where students are in their knowledge of the genre knowledge they will need in the summative assessment.		
• Analyze student work to identify what language to focus on in this unit.		
Building Knowledge of the Field		
• Research the topic through viewing, reading, discussing.		
• Weigh evidence, examine credibility of sources.		
• Watch videos with the purpose of deepening knowledge of the issue.		
• Design classroom discussions that allow students to consider different perspectives on the issue.		
• Teach students how to use graphic organizers to take notes on the learning as they research the topic.		
• Create anchor charts with key language students are noticing to indicate language of time, place, timelines.		
Supported Reading (see Chapter 5 or how this is done)		
• Set up structured conversations **about language** in the context of complex texts.		
• Paraphrase the text paragraph by paragraph to help students access the meaning of the text by looking at language. Paraphrasing allows students to focus on language without having to focus on content. It reduces cognitive load and frees up brain space to do the language work in the text.		

(Continued)

Table 4.1 (Continued)

Activities for each stage of the teaching and learning cycle	Self-assessment	
	I do this	Wondering about

- Identify key vocabulary in the context of text and how it represents key ideas throughout the text.
- Outline the text to teach the genre structure (Contributing Factors, Problems, Solutions) to access the deeper meaning of the text.
- Do **sentence-level language analysis** to look at language chunks and show students how language works within a sentence (e.g., participants, processes, and circumstances).

Modeling/Deconstruction

- Teach students the genre **by looking at language** to learn the genre and register features by attending to the following:
  - Structure of the whole text and how the text unfolds to meet its purpose,
  - Jobs of paragraphs and how they stack up to meet the purpose of the text,
  - Complex Noun groups and how they pack information,
  - Prepositional phrases of time and place,
  - Nominalization and how it repackages historic events into a noun,
  - Passive voice and how it hides agency, evades the blame, or avoids responsibility.

(Continued)

Table 4.1 (Continued)

Activities for each stage of the teaching and learning cycle	Self-assessment	
	I do this	Wondering about

Joint Construction

- Teacher and students write together a text in the same genre as the deconstructed text that matches the genre of the summative assessment. They negotiate together the language choices (not merely focusing on the content of the ideas, but discuss **how language works in text to create those ideas**. They use the following dialogic moves:
  - lead by shaping the text as it unfolds (e.g., *How should we construct a claim where we open spaces for other possibilities?*),
  - ask questions to solicit student responses (e.g., *Should we just should or have to here?*),
  - make suggestions (e.g., *How about we move this sentence to here?*),
  - recast as necessary (e.g., *You mean ...*), and
  - remind students of the stages, phases, and features of the deconstructed text (e.g., *How about providing some background before jumping into the discussion of the issue? Let's connect our ideas with more clarity. What text connective do we need here?*).

Independent Writing

- Students write independently using a checklist and a jointly constructed text as a model to follow the genre expectations.

Analysis and Reflection

- Teacher reviews student work in relation to the language functions and features identified and taught in the deconstruction stage.
- Teacher identifies patterns in student data and creates a plan to address them in the following unit (e.g., language for creating objective stance, language for creating the flow, language for stating claims without polarizing language, etc.).

Planning with the End in Mind

Planning with the End in Mind may be a familiar stage to you if you use a backward design approach. It is a stage in the instructional cycle where you would review standards and identify a summative assessment or a performance task that will be used to measure student learning at the end of the unit. Table 4.2 lists possible activities for this stage.

Mentor Texts (Model Texts)

One of the most important things you'll do in your journey to make language visible for your students is to write and/or analyze a mentor text, or model. The term "mentor text" is used in many ways in our field. The one we are referring to here has a very specific set of purposes for process and product. The *process* part is for you to walk in the shoes of your students, to enable you to make visible the language in the text for yourself so that you can plan what is needed to teach. The *product* you are looking for is a text that your students can write with your teaching and one that matches exactly what your assignment specifies, so it is a model student response, written like a student (not perfect like you). This need not be a daunting or time-consuming task.

To illustrate how useful mentor texts are for students, reflect on your experience as an adult, you might remember times when you also needed

Table 4.2 Planning with the End in Mind Stage: At a Glance

Planning with the End in Mind
• Identify standards addressed in the unit
• Identify a summative assessment that's connected to the central or compelling question in the inquiry
• Identify the genre of the summative assessment (e.g., explanations or arguments)
• Write a mentor text, or model, that matches the summative assessment
• Do a pretest to assess where students are in their knowledge of the genre they will need in the summative assessment
• Analyze student work to identify what language to focus on in this unit

a mentor text to learn from. Personally, we've needed mentor texts for the following types of writing:

- Writing bios for conference proposals
- Reviewing a product on Amazon
- Reviewing an academic book written for scholarly friends
- Writing a book chapter for this book
- Writing a recipe to share with friends how to bake sourdough

In the box below, list your tasks where you needed to look at a mentor text, similar to what we did above.

Tasks I needed mentor texts for in my personal or professional life:

1. _____

2. _____

3. _____

One of the most important criteria for choosing a mentor text is that it should match the genre of the summative assessment or your performance task. For example, if the summative assessment is a consequential explanation, then the mentor text also needs to be a consequential explanation. If you want your students to include a map along with a written explanation in the final performance task, then include a map in your mentor text. This approach of using a mentor text in social studies supports students because, as you will see in this chapter, it serves as a tool that makes explicit the expectations of the assessment prior to the students doing the assessment. As such, it is very different from what is typically done, where students are given an assignment and then set off on their own, which the teacher later scores with a rubric.

To write a good mentor text, you need to be crystal clear about your genre, the structure, and the language features. Use this book as your

Criteria for a mentor text	How you can use a mentor text
• Be written in student language • Be written with the same genre structure you are looking for • Contain language/grammatical features that are characteristic of the genre	• As a model to teach students how to write that genre • As a model to deconstruct with students to make visible the genre structure and language features • As a tool to analyze student work • As a tool for assessment

resource as well as your favorite social studies resources. Let's start with an inquiry unit and think about the tasks. This one is from the inquiry *Agriculture* for sixth grade from the C3 Framework. In this inquiry, students investigate the role of agriculture in the growth of complex ancient societies focusing on Mesopotamia.

C3 Inquiry 6th Grade: Agriculture[1]

Compelling Question: Was the development of agriculture good for humans?

Summative Task: Was the development of agriculture good for humans? Construct an argument (e.g., detailed outline, poster, or essay) that addresses the compelling question using specific claims and relevant evidence from historical sources while acknowledging competing views.

Supporting Questions:

1. How did environmental changes and new technologies affect the development of agriculture?
2. How did the development of agriculture in Mesopotamia lead to the development of writing?
3. What were the consequences of agriculture for humans?

Formative performance task: Develop a claim supported by evidence that agriculture had a range of consequences for human culture.

We are going to craft our mentor text to be one that responds to the Formative Performance Task. The reason for this, as opposed to writing one that would fit the Summative, is we want to create something that you can present to students for deconstruction and analysis. If you were to use the Summative prompt, then you would be giving students too much help and lose your assessment validity. There are four steps in the process of writing the mentor text. We will take you through this process one step at a time.

Step 1: Determine the Genre Structure and What Content Should Be Included

Your first step is to think through the genre stages and functions of the text you want your students to produce. You could use a table like the one below (Table 4.3). To figure out what stages and functions should be included in the task, refer back to Chapters 2 and 3 which lay out these for a variety of explanations and argument genres. It is particularly important to think about

Table 4.3 Genre Structure and Ideal Content

Genre stages and functions (jobs)	Ideal content for "What were the consequences of agriculture for humans?"
Orientation *Name the topic and give a brief explanation of the issue* Major Claim *Answer the question from the prompt in general terms. Make your statement of belief* Preview of the argument *Tell your reader what the two consequences you are going to write about are*	Topic: Agriculture in Mesopotamia • 12,500 BCE • Prior to the development, people were hunters and gatherers • Factors that contributed to the development (climate change, tools) • Beginning of civilization Claim: Consequences: • Disease • Wealth inequality
Continue with the rest of the Genre Stages and Jobs *(See Appendix for a longer example)*	Continue with the content that matches the Genre Stages and Jobs

the functions or jobs of the stages, as not only do these tell the students what to write, but they inform planning decisions on what language features need to be taught or employed.

Step 2: Drafting the Mentor Text to Align with Genre Stages and Functions (Jobs)

Once you have drafted the Genre Stages and Functions and made a quick outline of the content, draft your text in the middle column. (Note, you can skip this step of writing your own mentor text if you already have a text that fits the criteria above.)

Step 3: Analyzing the Mentor Text

Next is to analyze the text by looking for ways you used language features to express the functions of each stage. You can ask yourself questions like, 'How did I name the topic?' (I said Agriculture is ___). How did I organize the brief explanation? (I used logical connectors, before ... then). Don't worry too much about terminology with the language features, just try to get in the practice of paying attention to the choices you make when writing. Once you get really comfortable, you can do a second draft of the text, revising to add in language features that you think your students need to learn, for example, if you didn't put any text connectors in your first draft, add those in. You can consult Chapters 2 and 3 for the tables on language features that typically occur in the social studies genres. See Table 4.4 for an example of what we did.

Steps for Writing and Analyzing a Mentor Text

Step 1: Determine the Genre structure and what content should be included

Step 2: Draft the Mentor Text to Align with Genre Stages and Functions

Step 3: Analyze the text to determine which language features are important

Table 4.4 Drafting and Analyzing he Mentor Text to Align with Genre Stages and Functions

Genre stages and functions (jobs)	Draft Text "What were the consequences of agriculture for humans?"	Analysis: Key language features and sentence frames
Orientation Name the topic and give a brief explanation of the issue Major Claim Answer the question from the prompt in general terms. Make your statement of belief Preview of the argument Tell your reader what the two consequences you are going to write about are	Agriculture is when people grow their own food. People started doing this around 12,500 years ago. Before the development of agriculture, people were hunters and gatherers. Then, two things happened that changed this. One, it got warm enough for people to grow crops. Two, people learned to make tools, which helped them grow their crops. Then people didn't have to move around to find food, so they stayed in one place and built houses and made civilization. However, there are some consequences of agriculture. I will write about two bad consequences of agriculture. The first consequence is disease. The second consequence is some people got rich and others got poor	Sentence Frame: Agriculture is _____ (dependent clause) Time period Explanation sequences using logical connectors: *Before … then* Explanation is organized using text connectors: *two things, one … two* Cause-and-effect explanation sequence using logical connectors: *then … so* Transition from the explanation to the claim using a text connector: *however* Claim stated with a declarative sentence Preview using text connectors: *two … the first … the second* Sentence Frames: *The first consequence is* ___ *The second consequence is* ___

This table continues in the Appendix

The work you did on writing and analyzing the mentor text will yield many language features and genre organization structures. As you see from Table 4.4, there are a lot in the right-hand column. However, don't feel like you need to cover them all in one lesson. Narrow them down to 2–3 language features. One way to do this is to use your knowledge of your students past and present to determine likely areas they will need support. Another way to do it is to choose the ones that are within your comfort zone if you are new to this way of looking at language. When you choose the ones you are comfortable with, you are more likely to experience success, and that success may inspire you to take on new features in the future lessons. You'll want to aim for what most students will need support with, but you'll also want to think about differentiation. See below for more on differentiation. Another important tool you have to make these decisions is student reflection. As you and your students gain expertise in making language visible, students can decide what language features they want to work on. Student reflection on their own learning is crucial in developing the kind of awareness about language we are going for.

In this section we have shown you work that is critical to backward design planning, the writing and analysis of a mentor text. Incidentally, there are ways you can shortcut the actual writing of a mentor text by, for example, using a student piece from a previous year or a different class period. Additionally, at the time of this writing, ChatGPT was coming to the forefront. This tool may also be useful in creating mentor texts. Whether you write your own mentor text or not, we urge you to go through the work of analyzing it, as the work of analysis serves not just for planning, but will support your deconstruction and joint construction activities.

Building Knowledge of the Field

Building knowledge of the field is a stage that many of you may recognize and you may have identified in Table 4.1. It consists of activities that provide experiences, videos, research, class discussions designed to build conceptual knowledge on the topic. Table 4.5 provides a summary of the suggested activities for this stage.

This stage is important because it develops students' knowledge of the concept so that when they start working with the genre, they will have

Teaching and Learning Cycle for Disciplinary Genres

Table 4.5 Building the Field Stage: At a Glance

Building Knowledge of the Field

- Research the topic through viewing, reading, discussing
- Weigh evidence, examine credibility of sources
- Watch videos with the purpose of deepening knowledge of the issue
- Design classroom discussions that allow students to consider different perspectives on the issue
- Teach students how to use graphic organizers to take notes on the learning as they research the topic
- Create anchor charts with key language students are noticing to indicate language of time, place, timelines

developed a deep understanding of the issue or event they will be writing about. During this stage, the lenses of economy, geography, history, and politics can be brought in to develop students' multidimensional views of the issue.

> **In your Classroom:**
> Building the field is a stage many of you already do and may recognize through activities like:
>
> - Identify your compelling question worth pursuing through inquiry, which will guide student learning of the issue in the question.
>   - For example, in our unit, the question worth pursuing was *What was the impact of the forced relocation on the Ho-Chunk people?*
> - Design student interactions to take central stage with students talking to learn through their discussion of maps, videos, historical photographs, text, and other primary or secondary sources.
>   - For example, on the topic of the European settlement and the impact on the Ho-Chunk people, students will watch and discuss videos of historical accounts, cultural artifacts, first-person accounts, read and discuss primary sources such as maps of the Ho-Chunk territories of where they were forced to relocate.

- Carefully select a variety of multimodal sources to support students' learning of the topic such as videos, oral histories, maps, charts, and graphs. Explicitly teach students how to read multimodal texts and do not assume that just because it is an image or a map and not a language-heavy text, that students will know how to read a multimodal text.
  - In the Ho-Chunk unit, for example, you would explicitly teach students how to read maps that show the forcible removal of the Ho-Chunk as students continue to deepen their knowledge about this topic.

Supported Reading

The Supported Reading phase is all about teaching students how to read academic texts by taking a very close look at language and how language creates meanings in text. It's closely related to Building the Field because, through reading, students access content they then use for discussions and writing assessments. Table 4.6 lists a few selected activities to illustrate what we mean by teaching the language explicitly in the context of text.

Table 4.6 Supported Reading Stage: At a Glance

Supported reading stage activities
• Set up structured conversations about language in the context of complex texts. • Paraphrase the text paragraph by paragraph to help students access the meaning of the text by looking at language. Paraphrasing allows students to focus on language without having to focus on content. It reduces cognitive load and frees up brain space to do the language work in the text. • Identify key vocabulary in the context of text and how it represents key ideas throughout the text. • Outline the text to teach the genre structure (Contributing Factors, Problems, Solutions) to access the deeper meaning of the text. • Do sentence-level language analysis to look at language chunks and show students how language works within a sentence (e.g., participants, processes, and circumstances).

In a nutshell, this approach consists of the teacher guiding students through a text, as opposed to the teacher assigning a text for students to read independently. The texts that are part of the C3 Inquiries are inherently complex, and intentionally so. We want students to read authentic texts that are rich in content. Students need to read complex texts in order to make progress with academic reading. However, when we assign complex texts to students without providing support, we become part of the problem introduced in Chapter 1 by creating a situation where only some of our students get to fully participate. When most students are given texts they find too difficult to read, they simply will not read them. So we are left with an equity problem where some students read and get better at reading and others do not participate. In our research, we've seen social studies teachers try to get around this problem that the texts are too difficult for the majority of their students by not having students read at all, and these teachers find other ways to present the content. The Supported Reading stage of the TLC provides opportunities for you to scaffold complex texts in ways that enable all your students to make meaning. You can start by trying out the activities in Table 4.6. Additionally, Chapter 5 focuses on how to teach academic reading.

Text Deconstruction/Modeling: Language-Focused Conversations around Texts

The Text Deconstruction/Modeling phase is a phase that guides the students in learning about the social purpose of the genre, including the stages and phases of the text and how they unfold to achieve a text purpose. In other words, how are causal or consequential explanations structured and why? In our experience, we observed that students create timelines or answer comprehension questions at the end of the unit, or that writing was assigned but not taught. It is during the deconstruction stage when students are apprenticed into the genre of explanations or arguments in social studies. In a nutshell, deconstruction is the dedicated time in which you guide the students through activities that explicitly focus on the social purpose of the genre, including the genre stages (how the whole text is structured and why) and jobs of each stage, and/or the language features at the register level identified by yourself as part of your work in analyzing the mentor text. What students are deconstructing is the mentor text.

Deconstruction can last several lessons depending on the how familiar the students are with the genre you are asking them to produce. For example, if students never wrote a factorial explanation, you can plan 2–3 lessons to deconstruct the text to show the structure of the whole text and how it is different from merely narrating or recounting a series of historical events organized chronologically around a timeline. You can do this, for example, by:

- Designing a compare and contrast activity to build from the known to the new. Teaching students language of causality in explanations beyond *because* and *so* but other ways causality is expressed through *when*, *if* and *since* clauses and causal verbs *lead to, caused, brought about*.
- Teaching students how to identify passive voice and use of nominalization as described and illustrated in the previous chapter to uncover the human agency in the historical explanations.

Other activities you can try can involve manipulatives, physical movement, lining up the paragraphs, color coding, and others (Table 4.7).

Deconstruction can be best described as a guided conversation centered on text where you guide the students in noticing the language at the whole text, paragraph, sentence, and phrase levels (Table 4.7). During deconstruction, students learn that texts are not a "holy grail," some sacred vessel that holds something special and "untouchable," but that they were written by a human who made particular choices for a particular purpose, time, place, and audience. Even the number and order of the paragraphs is a choice, not just individual words that we often think of when we think of choices. Historical texts are mere interpretations, human understandings of events as they reconstruct from memory, and those reconstructions and interpretations are choices in and of themselves, as many history teachers will admit (Coffin, 2006). In addition, choices are made not only at the structural level but also at which events were included and which events were excluded, how people were named (settlers or colonizers), how the events were named (discovery or colonization), how events were nominalized to hide the agent (*the removal of children from their families*) when events were negative (the children *were sent away* to boarding schools) or reveal the agent when events were positive (*the settlers* greeted them kindly). Through these conversations,

Table 4.7 Activities for the Deconstruction Stage

Activities for the deconstruction stage

Purpose for deconstruction: to draw students' attention to the genre and language features in the text important to the genre.

Steps:
- Select/write/identify a mentor text.
- Analyze stages and features of text.
- Select 2–3 language features your students need.
- Select deconstruction activity, one for the whole text, and one for the sentence or phrase level.
- Plan the questions you'll ask your students to draw attention to the selected features.

Choices for Deconstruction Activities: Students can:

Whole text level/paragraph level
- Cut apart a text by stages and discuss the job of each stage.
- Mix them up and order them again and discuss why the author's choices.
- Move around hold chunks of text/pictures and discuss how to order themselves and why.
- Act out the different chunks of text/pictures to support comprehension.
- Restate text in their own words.

Sentence/phrase level:
- Color code noun groups, verbs, language of place and time, text connectives.
- Cut up the sentence by meaningful chunks.
- Mix up the phrases in the sentences.
- Act out the meanings.
- Talk about key vocabulary, passive voice, shades of meaning as they relate to your learning goals, suffixes, prefixes (word work).
- Talk about spelling, letter sounds, allow students to copy key language patterns – this will apprentice them to the structures of language that are key to the genre.
- Restate sentences in their own words.

---

students become critical thinkers when reading and informed choice-makers when writing.

Deconstruction is the necessary and often missing scaffolding in teaching disciplinary writing. In the text box below is a sample sequence you could use if you were to focus on the organization of the text:

In Your Classroom:

1. Allow students to order paragraphs of the mentor text and discuss the function of each paragraph.
2. Discuss organizational features and cohesive devices such as:
   - text connectives: *however, for example, although, despite, while,*
   - pronoun reference: *it, they, he,*
   - text reference: use of pronoun *this/that, these/those* as in *those actions led to the following consequences.*
3. Give students the structure of the genre. Color code various parts within paragraphs that students will need to include in their own writing:
   - sentence stating the consequence in red,
   - linking sentence or a linking word that refers back to a whole text chunk above in blue,
   - summary of consequences in yellow.
4. Students annotate the mentor text to explicitly see the structure and understand the purpose of each stage.

We want to voice that Deconstruction may feel new and awkward. One teacher had this to say about the Deconstruction: "It will feel like an overkill at first because this level of detail and conversation about text is not common and can feel unnecessary at first. We never teach this way! It feels like too much teaching. But trust the process, it's so worth it." It is important to recognize that, as with any new learning, there will be an awkward stage of adjusting to this approach, especially when it was not a common instructional practice before.

To reiterate, while deconstruction prepares students to learn the language of genre for writing, it is in these conversations around texts that students learn to notice the choices and the agendas behind those long and challenging historical texts; thus, they are learning how to become critical consumers of historical texts. Table 4.8 offers some guiding questions to illustrate what how to engage students during deconstruction of the mentor text. You are, of course, welcome to adjust these; however, we highly

Table 4.8 Questions to Ask Students during Deconstruction of Texts

Levels of language	Possible questions to ask your students
Whole Text Level **Purpose:** to identify social purpose of the genre and how the structure of the text supports the purpose	1. What's the purpose for this text? 2. How is the whole text organized to achieve its purpose? 3. Where have you seen texts like these? Show students several texts in the target genre. What do texts like these always/usually/sometimes have? 4. If we were to represent the ideas in this text as a graphic to show relationships between ideas, what would it look like? 5. How are these texts different from others (e.g., contrast historical narratives with explanations, both non-fiction texts, and yet they have a different organizational structure)?
Paragraph Level **Purpose:** to identify the job of the paragraph in the relation to the overall text	1. How many paragraphs are in the text and why? What is the job of each? 2. Which paragraphs are required/optional and why? 3. How are paragraphs connected from one to the other? If there are no connecting words, what is the glue that holds the text together?
Sentence Level **Purpose:** to identify the function of sentences	1. What is the job of the first sentence in each paragraph? (Let's call those paragraph openers because they open the paragraph by telling us what the paragraph will be about.) 2. How does the sentence add to our understanding of the content we are studying? 3. How can we say this sentence in our own words? 4. Can we divide this sentence into two or more sentences? What do we have to remove or change? 5. Can we say this sentence in a different order? How? 6. What other questions can we ask that will help us understand this sentence?

(Continued)

Table 4.8 (Continued)

Levels of language	Possible questions to ask your students
Phrase Level **Purpose:** to identify language features present in this genre	1. Who or what is this chunk about? What is the person or thing doing in this chunk? Where, where, and how? 2. What does this chunk tell us? Why do we think that? 3. How can we say this chunk in our own words? 4. Can we act out the chunk? Can we sketch the chunk? 5. Why did the author write this chunk? 6. What if we remove _____ in this chunk? Does it still make sense? Why do we think that? 7. What if we replace _____ in this chunk with _____? How does that change the meaning?

recommend they start with the whole text analysis to contextualize the rest of the language-focused conversation in a particular genre.

To further illustrate the process of deconstruction, we use some of the questions above and do a think-aloud using our mentor text we brought over from Chapter 2. The think-aloud will follow each level of text, starting with the whole text, down to paragraph level, to sentence and the phrase levels (Table 4.9).

Deconstruction of Orientation Paragraph

Another potential deconstruction activity is to focus students' attention on one paragraph. Let's now look at how we can deconstruct the introductory paragraph in our text called Orientation. Below is the first paragraph in our mentor text.

> <u>In Wisconsin in the late 1800s, many children of the Ho-Chunk nation were taken from their homes and sent away to boarding schools.</u> **The goal of these schools was assimilation, a political and social goal of the US government, designed to make the native American children learn the language and culture of the white people.** This had severe and lasting consequences on the Ho-Chunk community.

Teaching and Learning Cycle for Disciplinary Genres

Table 4.9 A Think-Aloud for Whole Text Deconstruction

Mentor text	Guiding questions to use during deconstruction
In Wisconsin in the late 1800s, many children of the Ho-Chunk nation were taken from their homes and sent away to boarding schools. The goal of these schools was assimilation, a political and social goal of the US government, designed to make the native American children learn the language and culture of the white people. This had severe and lasting consequences on the Ho-Chunk community. One consequence these boarding schools had was a disconnection of the children from the cultural ways of the Ho-Chunk which was achieved through systemic repression of the Ho-Chunk culture with particular focus on appearance, farming practices, and spiritual traditions. First, to make the Ho-Chunk children look more like white people, the teachers cut off the children's long hair. This was cruel because long hair was an intrinsic part of the children's identity as Ho-Chunk. Second, the children were taught that Ho-Chunk ways of farming were backward and forced to learn new ways of farming. The third example of repressing culture was with spiritual traditions. The children were taught Western religion in school. They were not allowed to practice Ho-Chunk spiritual traditions. Because the children had to cut their hair, learn new ways of farming, and a new religion, they ended up being disconnected from Ho-Chunk culture.	1. What's the purpose for this text? *The purpose is to explain what happened to the Ho-Chunk people because the kids got sent away to boarding schools.* 2. How is the whole text organized to achieve its purpose? *There are four paragraphs. The main event is at the beginning, then consequence 1 and consequence 2 and a summary at the end.* 3. Where have you seen texts like these? (Show students several texts in the target genre.) *We can find texts like these in blogs or textbooks. All texts have the main event at the beginning but some have three or four consequences. In videos and textbooks, there are the graphics and historic documents or photos too.* 4. What do texts like these always/usually/sometimes have? *Some texts leave out the evaluation at the end and invite the reader or viewer to draw their own conclusions. In textbooks, explanations are part of longer chapters which also include historical narratives and chronologies of events.*

(Continued)

Table 4.9 (Continued)

Mentor text	Guiding questions to use during deconstruction
The second consequence the boarding schools had on the Ho-Chunk was the loss of their language. At school, the children had to speak English. They were not allowed to speak Ho-Chunk language at all. This resulted in language loss which had the tragic effect of the children not being able to understand and not being able to connect with their elders when they eventually were allowed to return to their communities. Since they could not communicate with their elders, the children were unable to participate in the cultural practice of using stories to teach the children about their history and how to be a good member of the community. The consequence of sending Ho-Chunk children away to boarding school was a devastating loss of the Ho-Chunk culture and language. By not allowing the children to practice their culture, the result was the children forgot the culture or ended up preferring the white culture. By not allowing the children to speak Ho-Chunk language, the result was the children couldn't speak to or understand their elders, so they lost that connection to their historical traditions. Therefore, over time, the Ho-Chunk language was used by fewer and fewer children, and because of this, fewer adults.	5. If we were to represent the ideas in this text as a graphic, what would it look like? 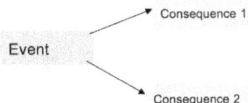 6. Which paragraphs are required/optional? Why? *This text has four paragraphs. The first one is important because it states the event. Without it, the other paragraphs would not make much sense. The summary paragraph is great but may be optional because in some cases, readers can draw their own conclusions.* 7. How does this text compare to recounts or historical narratives? *Recounts or narratives are organized around a sequence of events or chronologically.* *Consequential explanations are organized around an event and then the consequences with an evaluation or a summary at the end.*

The first paragraph is often called an introduction, and we often ask students to write an introduction, but what goes into an introduction remains a mystery. So, in the textbox below, we have identified and described sentence by sentence what this introduction includes. We call this stage orientation because we are orienting the reader to our text. In this consequential explanation, our introduction provides historic time and location, summarizes the event in one sentence, and tells the reader about what's coming next, which is the consequence.

<u>In Wisconsin in the late 1800s, many children of the Ho-Chunk nation were taken from their homes and sent away to boarding schools.</u> **The goal of these schools was assimilation, a political and social goal of the US government, designed to make the native American children learn the language and culture of the white people.** *This had severe and lasting consequences on the Ho-Chunk community.*	Introduce the event and the participants Provide historic time frame and location **Provide one-sentence summary of the event** *Introduce the consequences in general (without details and specifics) and let readers know what comes next*

Now let's take a look at what language features are in those sentences within orientation. Table 4.10 deconstructs the orientation by listing the function of each sentence, the language features, and the examples from our mentor text.

This level of detailed look at language within the introductory paragraph can better prepare students to understand what goes into an orientation. In this way, writing is scaffolded by taking the text apart in the context of the genre, looking at the whole text and each paragraph and what makes up a paragraph. One way you can use this table is to create an anchor chart to show how to write an Orientation paragraph. Another way is for students to use this as a guide to identify language they need for constructing their own paragraph.

Joint Construction

Joint construction is the next phase of the TLC following the deconstruction. Both of these phases are about genre work with the aim of apprenticing students into the curricular genre by learning how and why language

Table 4.10 Purpose of Orientation Paragraph and Language Features

Purpose of an orientation	Language features	Examples
Introduce the event and the participants	Noun groups	Many children of the Ho-Chunk nation
	Verb groups	*were taken* from their homes and *sent away* to boarding schools
Provide historic time frame and location	Prepositional phrase	In the late 1800s In Wisconsin
Provide summary of the event	Noun group	The goal of these schools
	Relating verb in past tense	was
	Nominalization with an embedded clause to define the event	assimilation, a political and social goal of the US government, designed to make the native American children learn the language and culture of the white people
Introduce the consequences in general (without details and specifics) and let readers know what comes next	Reference word to refer back to the event expanded noun group	**This** had severe and lasting consequences on the Ho-Chunk community

works in text. Joint Construction is a form of collaborative writing where students and you negotiate the meaning and create a shared text, but with a lot more talk about language in the context of text then you may be familiar with. We recommend beginning each Joint Construction activity with you holding the "pen" and inviting the students to contribute the language and content. Tables 4.11 and 4.12 illustrate what this might look like in a classroom.

Note, If we were doing this activity as part of our TLC-DG cycle, we would jointly construct a new piece of writing with a different topic but using the exact same generic structure and language features. For example, if the Ho-Chunk text was our mentor, we would jointly construct a text on a different consequence of Western Expansion, and then when students

Table 4.11 How to Do Joint Construction

How to do joint construction

1. Prepare materials:
   - Mentor text deconstructed showing stages and language features,
   - Anchor charts with language features.
2. Engage in students in **the following four steps**:
   - briefly review what students know about the genre,
   - orient the students to the writing task to be undertaken,
   - move into negotiating the joint text,
   - conclude with a reading of the complete text.
3. Spend most of the time on negotiating the joint text using some recommended Teacher Dialogic Moves.

TEACHER DIALOGIC MOVES

- lead by shaping the text as it unfolds (e.g., *Could we say that in fewer words?*),
- ask questions to solicit student responses (e.g., *Should we use passive or active voice here? Do we want our readers to know who did the action?*),
- make suggestions (e.g., *How about we move this sentence to here?*),
- recast as necessary (e.g., *You mean ...*), and
- remind students of the stages, phases, and features of the deconstructed text (e.g., *What do we need in the orientation? How do we indicate the language of time?*).

---

write their own text later they would do so on still a different consequence of Western Expansion.

Below, in Table 4.12, is an example of the classroom dialog that could occur around the joint construction of the Ho-Chunk text. We have labeled some of what the teacher is doing, try analyzing the rest yourself.

You may find that this phase resembles shared writing, a common approach to writing used in elementary schools; however, it has some distinct differences (see Table 4.13). The key difference is that instead of merely recording students' contributions, the teacher and the students together shape those contributions to resemble the features needed for the genre and register.

If we were to summarize Joint Construction in one sentence, we would say that it is a kind of dialogue between teacher and students consisting of talking and constructing the text together. An apt metaphor to describe joint

Table 4.12 Sample Dialogue between Teacher and Students Illustrating Joint Construction

The dialog	What the teacher is doing
4. T: What do we need in the orientation? 5. S1: Say stuff about the Ho-Chunk people	Reminding students of the stages and their functions from the deconstructed text (mentor text)
6. T: What exactly? 7. S1: Introduce the event and the Ho-Chunk people 8. T: Yes and what else? 9. S2: Tell about the time when it happened?	Asking questions to solicit student responses
10. T: Yes, we need a sentence to provide historic time frame to tell our readers those important time details. Let's look at our outline from yesterday here, and also let's look at our mentor text. How should we begin? 11. S3: They lived a long time ago. 12. T: Let's look at how the mentor text started 13. S1: Oh, we should start with the children … 14. **T: I agree, how about "Many children of the Ho-Chunk nation" …** 15. S1: Yeah 16. S2: We need to tell when it happened.	Drawing attention to the language features of the mentor text **Making suggestions**
17. **T: Excellent! Let's be specific about the historic timeline.** 18. S2: In the 1800s?	Drawing attention to the language features from the mentor text
19. T: Let's read what we have for our introduction. Who can find the language of time? 20. S3: I found it! "In the late 1800s!"	Asks questions to solicit responses

(Continued)

Table 4.12 (Continued)

The dialog	What the teacher is doing
21. T: Excellent let's write that. Now, what happened to the many children of the Ho-Chunk nation in the late 1800s? Keep reading the mentor text; find the verb group to tell what happened.	Drawing attention to the language features from the mentor text
22. S3: Reads "were taken from their families."	
23. T: Great suggestion. The question guys is whether we should name the doer – who took the children from their families? Right now do we know who took them if we say "were taken," is it passive or active voice?	
24. S3: Passive. It doesn't say who took them.	
25. T: The choice is yours. Do you want to name the doer or focus on what happened to the children and not on who took them?	
26. S4: Hmmm, let's name who took them.	
27. S3: But we are focusing on the children and not on the government.... This is hard ...	
28. T: Ok, let's make a decision. What is the job of this paragraph?	
29. S5: Introduce the event and the participants and tell about the consequences.	
30. S5: Then should we should focus on the consequences.	
31. T: Excellent discussion. Turn and talk to your elbow partner about what you think we should write for this sentence.	

Table 4.13 Shared Writing versus Joint Construction

Shared writing	Joint construction
The purpose is to create a text with students to serve a content goal. For example, shared writing on an introduction.	To lead the students to write a text using the patterns and language features observed in Deconstruction.
Students provide suggestions and content and the teacher writes it down.	Students' contributions during JC are oral, shaped by the teacher to approximate academic written-like language. The key difference is to translate spoken language into written language.
Teacher role: To record student ideas.	**Teacher role:** Recasting, paraphrasing, thinking aloud, including elaborating and restating to craft students' contributions to match the desired genre.

construction would be that of apprenticeship, a stage of learning where the master chef and the apprentices cook together with the chef leading and doing the teaching and the necessary adjustments to allow the students learn the art and science of a new dish before they are expected to enter a competition for the best desert. As in trades, joint construction is something students do several times with their teacher before they perfect their skills. It is not a one-time occurrence after which the students are expected to succeed independently. Table 4.14 provides a nice summary, including steps of how to do it, how to relate to Deconstruction, teacher and student moves to set up true dialogic teaching.

Right before students start writing independently after they jointly constructed the text, it is a perfect time to jointly construct the checklist that students will later use to guide their writing (see Table 4.15 for an example).

Independent Construction with Support as Needed

After Deconstruction and Joint Construction, the students are now ready to write their own texts on a different topic but in the same genre. Even though it is called independent construction, some students will still need

Teaching and Learning Cycle for Disciplinary Genres

Table 4.14 Joint Construction: At a Glance

Joint construction[2]

WHAT IS IT?

- A special kind of dialogue between teacher and students with students and teacher negotiating language choices together.
- A strongly framed activity where the teacher takes a dominant role.
- Is a critical stage in the teaching and learning cycle, where the teacher leads the students to write a whole text (in a topic similar but not identical to that which the students will later write independently).
- Consists of the following kinds of dialogic moves by teacher and students:
    - Teacher: questions, paraphrases, recasts, thinks aloud (elaborating, restating), makes statements
    - Students: compose content, make comments, question
- Is connected to Deconstruction because the teacher draws attention to the patterns and language features observed in the previous stage.
- Students may return to building the field, ensuring that they have sufficient background knowledge to contribute to the joint construction and that information gathered is organized visibly in a way that anticipates the genre to be jointly constructed.
- Students contribute their understandings, while the teacher scribes these in a way that supports the joint construction.
- Most work is done in the negotiating stage, the length of which varies according to the age and experience of the students. If texts are often too long to be jointly constructed in one lesson, then jointly construct a few sections such as the opening paragraph, and take several sessions to jointly construct the rest.
- Joint construction can be started as a whole class and moved into small groups with students who need more support working with the teacher at a table.

support from peers or yourself. During this phase, students should be using a checklist that they have co-constructed with you at the end of the Joint Construction phase.

Analysis of and Reflection on Student Work

This section builds out the last component of the Teaching Learning Cycle: Analysis of and Reflection on Student Work. We begin by showing you how to analyze samples of student-work with the purpose of informing your

Table 4.15 Writing a Consequential Explanation Student Checklist

Name: _____ Date: _____
Title of your piece: _____

Genre stages and functions	Structure	Language features
Input/Orientation Job of this stage: identify historical situation or event leading to change	I introduced the events and the participants I provided historic timeframe and location I provide summary of the event I introduced the consequences in general (without specific details) and let the reader know what comes next	____ I used expanded noun groups "children of the Ho-Chunk nation" to specify people ____ I used prepositional phrases to indicate a time frame and place e.g., in Wisconsin in the late 1800s ____ I used an expanded noun group to define and provide details about the event "assimilation, which means"…
Consequence 1 Job of this stage: elaborate on the effects of the event	____ I stated the consequence ____ I gave 2–3 examples ____ I elaborated on the effects of the event	I made choices to show how my text is organized ____ e.g., *One consequence* or *The first consequence* or *First,* ____ I used a nominalization to state the consequence (e.g., *a disconnection*) ____ I used verbs and other language resources to state effects *resulted in, led to, contributed to* … ____ I used noun groups to elaborate "negative consequences" and ____ I used prepositional phrases to specify time and location

(Continued)

Table 4.15 (Continued)

Name: _____ Date: _____		
Title of your piece: _____		
Genre stages and functions	Structure	Language features
Consequence 2 Job of this stage: elaborate on the effects of the event	____ I told the reader the second consequence I elaborated on the effect/consequence	____ I made choices to show how my text is organized e.g., *Another consequence* or *The second consequence* ____ I used noun groups to pack in detail (e.g., *systemic repression of the Ho-Chunk culture*) ____ I used nominalization to state the effect e.g., *the loss* (versus *when they lost their language, it had these effects ...*)
Reinforcement of consequences Job of this stage: emphasize and/or evaluate consequences	____ I summarized briefly without repeating information from the previous paragraphs ____ I provide an evaluation of the consequences	____ I used an expanded noun group to summarize and restate the consequences (e.g., *The consequences of sending Ho-Chunk children away to boarding school*) ____ I use evaluative adjectives e.g., *a devastating loss ...*

planning. Then we show you how to use the data from the analysis to plan differentiated instruction. We conclude with a plug to get students being involved in the reflection on their data, which develops student agency and can contribute to motivation and investment in their own learning.

Collecting Student Work to Inform Planning

The purpose of collecting and analyzing student work is to inform planning and to reflect on how students are learning. Ideally, the collection would work like this: You would assign your students a short writing piece that has the same prompt as the mentor text you have worked on. So in the case of the example on the 6th grade agriculture inquiry, the prompt would be: "What were the consequences of agriculture for humans?" Shorten the assignment if needed so students can write in class for one class period, for example, have them write just two paragraphs instead of five. Time the assignment so that students have already done the reading and can refer to the texts, but before you do the Deconstruction work on the mentor text and before you get into your explicit teaching about the genre. If you are using one of the C3 Inquiries, it makes sense to use one of the formative assessment prompts, with the idea being that you will explicitly teach what students need to know to write the Summative piece but that they will write that one with less support. Remind students of the reading they did and suggest that they use that for evidence in their arguments.

> **Tips for Collecting Student Work:**
> You may be worried about disrupting the flow of the lesson sequence by stopping to have students write something you can analyze. Here are some ideas:
>
> 1. Build in this time for student writing into your lesson planning. In this chapter, we used one of the formative assessments as part of the Inquiry; you could build in the writing as a longer Exit Ticket.
> 2. Shorten the assignment to where the students will write just one paragraph, pick one that will give you the most bang for your buck, like the Consequence one paragraph we focus on here, or an explanation sequence like the one in the Orientation.
> 3. Use previous students' writing. Save a sample of your current year's students Summative Performance Task writing for analysis for next year (students will be different, but there will likely be similarities in what students can do and need support doing). A clear benefit to do it this way is that you can do this work before your unit begins.

Analyzing Student Work to Inform Planning

The idea and purpose behind analyzing student work is to figure out which of the genre stages, functions and language features students will need support on. The goal is to focus on how the students use language to express their content and disciplinary understanding. There are many ways to go about this. Here is one way that we've found to be helpful and efficient:

1. Quickly read through a class set of papers and divide them into High, Medium, and Low based on quick impressions.
2. Select one high, one medium, and one low paper.
3. Analyze three papers.
4. Make copies of the three papers so you can return them to students without your analysis notes.

To figure out what you are looking for in the student work, you may want to look back at your mentor text analysis (see Table 4.4). In addition, if you've done a Student Checklist, you could look at that too (see Table 4.15) Start your analysis by identifying how the students expressed the genre stages and note whether or not they realized the function. Then analyze how the students used language features to realize the function. Highlight, underline, mark up the papers. Collect data. Look for trends. We will show you how next.

We will now look at three samples of student writing. Imagine these three sixth graders, Ira, Lucas, and Carlos, wrote these *after* they learned and discussed the content but *before* they have received any explicit teaching on language for writing an argument using a Claim, Evidence, and Reasoning structure. Here is the prompt the teacher used to invite the students to write the sample she collected:

> **Teacher:**
> We have been learning a lot about the development of agriculture in Mesopotamia. We looked at a graph and some pictures yesterday and discussed how there were some consequences that happened because of agriculture. Today, we are going to do a quick write to give me an idea about what you know about writing an argument. Let's read the prompt together:

What were the consequences of agriculture for humans?

Now, you are going to write one paragraph. Your goal is to develop a claim supported by evidence that the development of agriculture had consequences for humans.

Imagine you are Ira, Lucas, and Carlos' teacher. Here is what you collected. Recall that the mentor text analyzed in the beginning of this chapter responded to this same prompt. See Appendix for complete text. Note that the students are already familiar with the pieces of evidence, the graph, and the pictures. As you read, think about what these students know about a Claim, Evidence, and Reasoning structure:

Ira's Argument

Agriculture had consequences for human culture. One consequence was pandemics. Many people got sick and died. We learned this was because people were living together in towns, and that's why they got sick. If there wasn't agriculture, there would be no pandemics.

Lucas's Argument

I think agriculture was bad because many people died. Why did people die? People died because they were living close together in towns, and there were viruses they got. They didn't have any vaccinations. Before agriculture, people moved around hunting and gathering. They didn't get sick.

Carlos' Argument

It was not a good idea to do agriculture. The evidence is on the graph. The death rates go up when there is a pandemic or famine. I think people died because of the pandemic and famine.

> **Try this out:** What are your initial impressions of these paragraphs? How well did the students address the prompts? Compare these pieces with the mentor text from Part 1 in this chapter (full text in the Appendix)
>   Questions to ask:
> - What do these students already know about this specific type of writing I am asking them to do?
> - What do they not know?
> - What will they need support in doing?
>
> If you have a rubric you use for arguments, go ahead and use it.
>   Rate the paragraphs from 1–3. Compare and discuss with a thought partner.

Next we will show you how we analyzed the three student texts by focusing on the genre structure and language features used to realize the jobs of each genre stage.

Ira's Writing

Agriculture had consequences for human culture. One consequence was pandemics. Many people got sick and died. We learned this was because people were living together in towns and that's why they got sick. If there wasn't agriculture, there would be no pandemics.

	Notes:
☑ Writing claims with declarative sentences *Agriculture had consequences for human culture.* ☐ Explicitly referring to evidence e.g., "The graph shows ___" ☑ Logical connectors that express cause and effect e.g., "that's why," "therefore," and "because"	• Ira makes a major claim and a first consequence claim. • She has conceptual understanding of what she is claiming as evidenced with her referencing the pandemic and also with this sentence here: *We learned this was because people were living together in towns and that's why they got sick.*

(Continued)

We learned this was because; that's why; If there

☐ Logical connectors that express before and after e.g.,: "before," "then"

☐ Explicitly referring to the reasoning section "This shows that ____"

☑ Descriptive language with noun phrases with describing words and clauses
got sick and died

- However, she did not refer to a specific piece of evidence. She could be thinking about the graph and not referring to it or she could be thinking about a class discussion on the graph.
- She is missing logical connectors related to time, like before, after and then which would help her express the connection between the pandemic and the development of agriculture.
- She is also weak in expressing the causal relationship between the development of agriculture and disease.
- She does use the logical connectors *that's why* and *if then* but without the before and after logical connection, her last two sentences don't achieve her purpose.
- Focus on stating the evidence and logical connectors. Sentence frames with logical connectors would also probably help.

Lucas' Writing

I think agriculture was bad because many people died. Why did people die? People died because they were living close together in towns and there were viruses they got. They didn't have any vaccinations. Before agriculture, people moved around hunting and gathering. They didn't get sick.

☑ Writing claims with declarative sentences

An opinion is stated: *I think agriculture was bad because many people died,* but not in the form of a declarative statement.

☐ Explicitly referring to evidence e.g., "The graph shows ____"

Other notes on the Analysis:

- Overall, this reads more like an explanation about why people died during Neolithic times than an argument that the development of agriculture had consequences.

(Continued)

Teaching and Learning Cycle for Disciplinary Genres

- ☑ Logical connectors that express cause and effect e.g.,: "that's why," "therefore," and "because"
  Why? ... because
- ☐ Logical connectors that express before and after e.g.,: "before," "then"
- ☐ Explicitly referring to the reasoning section "This shows that _____"
- ☑ Descriptive language with noun phrases with describing words and clauses
  living close together in towns, viruses, vaccinations

- Lucas does not begin with a clear declarative statement claim.
- He does not refer to evidence, but perhaps a class discussion.
- The cause-and-effect reasoning about why people got sick is expressed through logical connectors.
- Focus on: Writing a claim, naming and describing evidence.

Try it out: Analyze Carlos' paragraph using the table below. Think about what you would focus on to support him. See the Appendix Answer Key if needed.

Carlos' Writing

It was not a good idea to do agriculture. The evidence is on the graph. The death rates go up when there is a pandemic or famine. I think people died because of the pandemic and famine.

- ☐ Writing claims with declarative sentences
- ☐ Explicitly referring to evidence e.g., "The graph shows ___"
- ☐ Logical connectors that express cause and effect e.g.,: "that's why," "therefore," and "because"
- ☐ Logical connectors that express before and after e.g.,: "before," "then"
- ☐ Explicitly referring to the reasoning section "This shows that _____"
- ☐ Descriptive language with noun phrases with describing words and clauses

Notes:

Moving from Analysis of Student Work to Planning

Though we only looked at three student paragraphs, patterns emerged in areas where students need support in crafting their argument. The major area, and this comes as no surprise for sixth graders, is understanding what is different between an argument and explanation. This needs to be understood both conceptually, meaning arguments express ideas with claims, evidence and reasoning and explanations use cause and effect (in addition to other ideas) and practically, meaning how to do this with language. We saw this with Lucas and Carlos and to a lesser extent with Ira. The lack of explicitly referring to evidence, both naming it and describing it was a pattern as was writing a claim in declarative form. In addition, while arguments will all have cause-and-effect explanation sequences that need logical connectors, some content dictates certain types of logical connections. In this case, the topic of the development of agriculture having consequences calls for language that expresses what happened before and what happened after, likely all students will need support with this.

Overall, these are the areas students need support:

- Writing claims with declarative sentences
- Explicitly referring to evidence
- Logical connectors that express cause and effect: *that's why, therefore,* and *because*
- Logical connectors that express before and after: *before, then*
- Explicitly referring to the reasoning section using *This shows that*

- Improving descriptive language by building noun phrases with describing words and clauses

Using Student Data to Inform Instruction

After analyzing student data, we would narrow down to 2–3 to focus on. Then we would design learning targets to address them, for example,

1. Learning Target: I can write a claim about the consequences of agriculture using a declarative sentence.

2. Learning Target: I can express my reasoning using *This shows that* _____.

3. Learning Target: I can use logical connectors that express cause and effect including: *that's why, therefore,* and *because*.

The important point is you can't and don't have to teach everything that you know your students need and/or what you discovered about the text from doing an analysis of a mentor text. By doing this work of analysis, you'll be prepared to lead your students through a series of Deconstruction and Joint Construction activities during the Teaching Learning Cycle that will support them in their argument writing. In addition, this analysis work leads right into some clearly targeted differentiation.

Planning for Differentiation

We look at students' need for differentiation to be temporary, meaning what one student needs a lot of help with in writing arguments, they may not need much help writing an explanation. We distinguish between three types of differentiation: "lighter support" which refers to supports designed for enrichment; "moderate support" refers to the kind of support most students need, delivered as a whole class; "heavier support" supports designed to be delivered in small groups or with individuals.

Here are some examples of supports we designed for this agriculture task for/with lighter, moderate, and heavier support.

For lighter support: Provide students with their own copies of the mentor text. Students can practice substituting in alternative logical connectors. They can use *for example* in strategic places in the text to add more content to the explanations. Students can begin crafting counterarguments to add to the mentor text or their own drafts.

For moderate support: Whole class deconstruction and joint construction activities. In addition, support students in writing an explanation sequence using a Mad Libs/something. Example: Before *the development of agriculture* _____ (what happened?) _____. Then (what happened to cause the change?) *two things happened. One* (explain thing one). *Two* (explain thing two).

Support students in using logical connectors by creating a bank. Example:

Logical Connectors that have to do with time:	Logical connectors that show one thing caused another:
Before ... then ... after	Because
_____ at the same time _____	As a result
Etc.	That's why
	Etc.

For heavy support: It may be overwhelming to write an argument with two argument paragraphs. Students can write one. Help them decide by discussing the evidence and talking through how it supports their claim. One piece of evidence will likely stick out. Provide students with sentence frames. Examples:

The consequence of the development of agriculture is _____
The graph/piece of evidence shows _____
This evidence shows us _____

Student Reflection on Their Own Work

With your guidance, students can reflect on their use of language and understanding of the genre they need to produce. The ideal time for reflection would be after Deconstruction in the Teaching Learning Cycle. Deconstruction is when you present your students with your mentor text and show how you analyzed it and what language features are important. Here is a sample script of what this might look like the following in the textbox below:

Teacher Reflection on the Task (Prior to Doing Their Own Writing)

Teacher: Yesterday we looked at our mentor text on the consequences of agriculture. Who can tell us what genre we decided would be best to use to respond to the prompt?
Students: Argument
Teacher: That's right, why?

> Students: Because the prompt said we had to do a claim and evidence and that's what arguments do.
> Teacher: Right, [display the chart with the text in the middle and genre stages and functions on the left and grammatical features on the right] Let's read through this table and remind ourselves of what we discovered about what we need to do with our language to meet the purpose of these stages and functions. [read through table with students]
> Teacher: Now let's think about your own writing. You are going to write a text just like this one. What do you think would be easy to do?
> Students: [Responses will vary but may include ...] using the sentence frames like, "this shows that"; saying what the consequence is.
> Teacher: Good, now what do you think would be difficult? Remember, what one person finds easy, another person may find difficult. Also because something seems difficult now, doesn't mean it always will. I am asking this because I want to make sure I teach you all what you need to know.
> Students: [Responses will vary but may include ...] writing the reasoning part; how to do dependent clauses.
> Teacher: Ok, now turn and talk to a partner about what you think may be difficult and easy. Then I'm going to have you fill out an Exit Ticket where you will write one thing that you think is going to be easy and one thing you think will be difficult. I am going to take these and use them for my planning to make sure that I teach you what you need to know.

The important point about this reflection is to involve students in the planning; it's a language-focused way of asking students what they want to learn. It promotes metacognitive awareness about what we need to do about how we do things with language to meet certain functions and that we can be taught how to do these things. Note that there are three opportunities for students to reflect. The first is the whole class discussion; the second is the turn-and-talk partner discussion; and the third is the Exit Ticket. This structure is intentional in that it ensures that all voices are heard.

Student reflection on work they have produced: This is a reflection you could do after the students have written a formative piece of writing.

The purpose of this is twofold: One is to inform your planning particularly how you will differentiate; the second is to share ownership of the learning with the students.

Here is how you could do this:

- Provide students with copy of the mentor text chart and their own piece of ungraded writing.
- Invite students to compare their piece with the mentor text and notice similarities and differences.
- Focus on language more than content. Invite students to reflect on how they used the sentence frames and grammatical features to meet the functions. Invite them to jot down 1–2 areas where they think they could use more support.

This is a task that invites differentiation. Here are two ways:

> Invite students to reflect on their pieces using the following prompts:
> - Underline all the sentence frames you used from the mentor text chart. How could you say those in a different way?
> - Where in your argument could you elaborate using *because* ____? Make a note of that.
> - Where in your argument could you add in a sentence that starts with *for example* ____?

Student Reflection with Heavier Support

Scaffold the reflection as needed. For example:

Teacher: Let's read the first paragraph of our mentor text. We noticed that this text starts with a statement that tells us what our topic is and uses the structure *Agriculture is* ____. Now look at your writing. Did you also use that sentence starter in your writing? Underline it.

> Teacher: Now let's look at the claim statement in the second paragraph. If we look at the genre stage and function, it tells us what we are supposed to do here. Who can remind us?
> Student: [looking at the mentor text chart] Tell the reader what your first consequence is.
> Teacher: Right, now what kind of language can we use to do that?
> Student: [looking at the mentor text chart] We can say the first consequence is ____.
> Teacher: That's right, take a look at your second paragraph, did you tell your reader what the first consequence is? Underline that. If you didn't, that's ok, just make a note on your paper to remind yourself to do that.
>
> Continue on as appropriate, guiding students through the piece, and then invite them to jot down one or two things they need support with.

Summary

In this chapter, we explained and illustrated an apprenticeship pedagogy for teaching writing in the disciplines called the Teaching and Learning Cycle. Here are the main reasons why we are calling an apprenticeship pedagogy and why we chose this pedagogy in our pursuit of equity.

1. It positions students as knowers and builds up their knowledge of three things simultaneously: Content knowledge, genre knowledge, and register (language knowledge).
2. It does not assume that students know how to write just because they learned the content but explicitly teaches students curricular genres in highly scaffolded ways.
3. It demystifies expectations for what the student writing should look like by asking teachers to write their own mentor texts to develop empathy and be clear what is expected of students.
4. It validates students' contributions and extends their linguistic repertoires by carefully crafting them together.

Notes

1 https://c3teachers.org/inquiries/agriculture/
2 Based on Derewianka & Jones (2023). *Teaching language in context* (3rd ed.). Routledge.

Reference

Coffin, C. (2006). *Historical discourse: The language of time, cause, and evaluation*. Continuum.

Chapter 4 Appendix

Table 4.4 continued: Analyzing the text to determine which language features are important

Genre Stages and Functions (Jobs)	Text "What were the consequences of agriculture for humans?"	Key grammatical features and Sentence Frames
Orientation Name the topic and give a brief explanation of the issue Major Claim Answer the question from the prompt in general terms. Make your statement of belief	Agriculture is when people grow their own food. People started doing this around 12,500 years ago. Before the development of agriculture, people were hunters and gatherers. Then, two things happened that changed this. One, it got warm enough for people to grow crops. Two, people learned to make tools, which helped them grow their crops. Then people didn't have to move around to find food, so they stayed in one place and built houses and made civilization.	Sentence Frame: Agriculture is _____ (dependent clause) Time period Explanation sequences using logical connectors: before … then Explanation is organized using text connectors: two things, one … two Cause-and-effect explanation sequence using logical connectors: then … so Transition from the explanation to the claim using a text connector: however

(Continued)

Teaching and Learning Cycle for Disciplinary Genres

Table 4.4 (Continued)

Preview of the argument Tell your reader what the two consequences you are going to write about are	However, there are some consequences of agriculture. I will write about two bad consequences of agriculture. The first consequence is disease. The second consequence is some people got rich and others got poor.	Claim stated with a declarative sentence Preview using text connectors: two … the first … the second Sentence Frames: *The first consequence is* ___ *The second consequence is* ___
Consequence 1 (Claim 1): *Tell your reader the first consequence* Evidence: *Give evidence from one of the sources that gives more detail and examples about your claim* **Reasoning: *Tell your reader how the evidence shows that your claim is right (how evidence supports claim)***	The first consequence is disease. The graph shows us that before agriculture started, people lived and died in a normal pattern. Then when agriculture started there was a pandemic and lots and lots of people died. Then there was a famine and more people died. **This evidence shows us that disease and death happened at the same time that agriculture developed. That's why disease and death are a bad consequence of agriculture.**	Claim stated with declarative sentence Name the piece of evidence: *The graph* Explanation sequence describing the graph. Logical connectors *Before … then … then* Descriptive language: *Lots and lots of people died* (expanded noun phrase) Cause-and-effect explanation sequence Logical connector of correlation: *at the same time* Logical connector of cause and effect: *that's why* Use of the verb *shows*: *The graph shows* *The evidence shows* Sentence Frames: Claim: *The first consequence is* ___ Evidence: *The graph shows us that* ___ Reasoning: *This evidence shows us that* ___

(Continued)

Table 4.4 (Continued)

Consequence 2 (Claim 2): *Tell your reader the second consequence* Evidence: Give evidence from one of the sources that gives more detail and examples about your claim **Reasoning: *Tell your reader how the evidence shows that your claim is right (how evidence supports claim)***	The second consequence is that some people got rich and others got poor. <u>One picture we looked at showed us a grass hut that people lived in before the development of agriculture. After agriculture it was different. The other picture shows us this. There is a white house and inside there are lots of things that the people had like bowls and blankets and decorations.</u> **This is evidence that the people who lived in the house had things that were just for them and not for sharing. We can imagine that some people had more things and others had less and they didn't share anymore. This shows that agriculture was the beginning of some people being rich and others poor.**	Claim stated with declarative sentence Name the evidence: *one picture, the other picture* Explanation sequence describing the pictures. Logical connectors: *before, after* Descriptive language: *Lots of things that people had like bowls and decorations and blankets. and inside in* (expanded noun phrase) Cause-and-effect explanation sequence Dependent clauses to add detail and repetition: *that were just for them and not for sharing; and they didn't share anymore* Logical connector of cause and effect: *this shows that* Cohesion created using *This* Sentence Frames: Claim: The first consequence is _____ Evidence: The other picture shows _____ Reasoning: This is evidence that _____ This shows that _____

(*Continued*)

Table 4.4 (Continued)

Restatement of position Give an opinion about why the topic is important Try to be friends with the reader Say your claims again	The development of agriculture was a really important time in human history. We needed it for civilization. But, not everything that happened as a result of agriculture was good. There were two bad consequences, disease, and social inequality, which is when some people are rich and others are poor.	Evaluative language *Really important* Including the reader using *We* Arguing with the reader *Not everything that happened was good*

Chapter 4 Answer Key

Carlos' Writing
It was not a good idea to do agriculture. The evidence is on the graph. The death rates go up when there is a pandemic or famine. I think people died because of the pandemic and famine.

- Writing claims with declarative sentences
It was not a good idea to do agriculture.
- Explicitly referring to evidence e.g., 'The graph shows ___'
The evidence is on the graph, The death rates go up when there is a pandemic or famine.
- Logical connectors that express cause and effect, e.g., : 'that's why', 'therefore', and 'because'
when ... because
- Logical connectors that express before and after e.g.,: "before," "then"
- Explicitly referring to the reasoning section "This shows that _____"
I think people died because of the pandemic and famine. (Missing a connection back to the claim)
- Descriptive language with noun phrases with describing words and clauses
pandemic and famine

Notes:
- Carlos makes a claim, but needs revision to make it more formal and to include the word "consequences" which is from the prompt.
- He refers to a piece of evidence and describes the evidence.
- He uses a cause-and-effect sequence to explain the relationship between death rates and pandemic and famine, which is on the graph.
- He begins to do some reasoning but needs to make a connection between the evidence and the claim.
- Focus on: Writing a more formal claim, using sentence frames to support the reasoning section.

A Language-Based Approach to Disciplinary Reading

Introduction

In the previous chapter, we identified the problem that many students in our social studies classrooms cannot read the complex texts we assign to them. We called upon you to take up this issue and provide the support your students need in order to read these texts. We promise we will describe a variety of ways you can do this, but first we need to dig into the problem a little more. The reasons your students cannot read your texts are incredibly complex, and we have chosen two of the factors to focus on. We think that not only are these factors most relevant to your work, but they are ones you can address in your classroom.

> ### Why Do Many Students Struggle to Read Complex Academic Text?
>
> Factor 1: Lack of student participation and engagement in reading instruction caused by systemic racism in education
>
> Factor 2: Approaches to teaching reading that fragment the components of the reading process

Lack of Student Participation in Reading Instruction

School learning takes place task by task, with each task a building block upon which to place the next block. Imagine a tower of blocks; this represents academic achievement. If students do not complete the task,

DOI: 10.4324/9781003302711-5

they do not get to place the next block. Let's call this "not learning." "Not learning" in one class period can lead to "not learning" in the next class period, and so on, until the "not learning's" become their own sets of building blocks, but instead of building a tower, students are digging a hole, with each "not learning" representing a shovel of dirt. When the hole gets too deep, the student can't climb out of it.

This metaphor of some students building towers and others digging holes is a useful way to think about academic achievement. It is not a perfect metaphor, though, because it implies that the students get to decide whether they build a tower or dig a hole. This is not always the case. Who are the students who get to decide whether to build a tower or a hole? Who doesn't get to choose? And why? When not everyone builds towers, we have an equity problem because it means that not everyone is empowered to go build the next tower, and thus not everyone achieves academically on par with everyone else. The role systemic racism plays is to prevent students from having the blocks to begin with, not just once, but time after time. Victims of systemic racism do not get to choose whether to build a tower or a hole, they are forced into digging holes.

Here is what this can look like in schools. The story is about Darius,[1] a smart, funny Black fourth-grade boy, in a mostly White suburban elementary school. This is a true story that took place during one of our research projects where we researchers became teachers and every day, for six weeks, we used the Teaching and Learning Cycle to teach the writing block in Darius' class (Westerlund & Besser, 2021). Every day, we struggled to engage and include Darius in our whole class lessons. His regular teacher had to sit next to him with her arms around him to get him to stay present. He would let her do this for a while, but seven times out of ten, he would lose his temper and storm out of the room. On one particular day, as he stormed out, we could hear him yelling in the hall, "I hate this f ***ing white school!"

Up until that point, we hadn't really framed our struggles in getting him to participate as being related to racism. But as we dug into this and talked to his teachers, we learned that since he began school, his teachers had struggled to get him to "behave appropriately," and that since Kindergarten he has spent the majority of each school day outside of the classroom in the common area working independently, often with a teacher sitting next to him. It was in this manner, with either one of us or his teacher sitting next to him, outside the room, that Darius wrote a literary response essay and showed us how capable he really was.

Disciplinary Reading

We came to understand that Darius' behavior patterns were likely triggered responses to repeated messaging he received that told him that he didn't belong, that he wasn't sitting nicely like the other kids, that he wasn't learning to read or write like the other kids, that he wasn't smart like the other kids. It would have been easy for Darius to see that the kids who were doing it right were the White kids, and since he wasn't a White kid, he would never get it right. The only times he was able to accomplish tasks and stack blocks on top of each other was when he was working one-to-one with teachers. But each day something would trigger him and he would knock down the tower and start digging holes. What will happen to Darius in middle and high school, when he's not surrounded by caring teachers who have the time and patience to support him? In fact, we've seen many Darius' in middle and high school. We've seen them out on the corner smoking weed before school, in remedial classes, getting kicked out of regular classes, or storming out themselves.

Now, let's imagine Darius is in your 10th grade World History class. How are you going to get him to build a tower?

Approaches to Teaching Reading that Fragment the Components of the Reading Process

Let's look again at this model from Chapter 1 (Figure 5.1). See below.

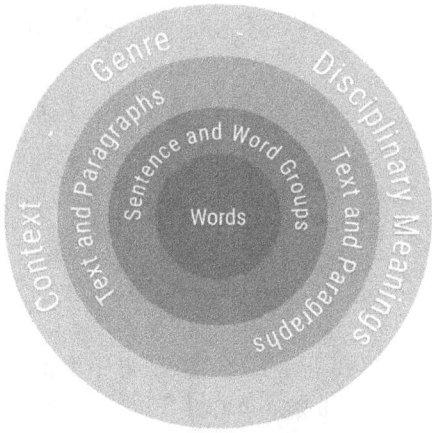

Figure 5.1 A Stratified model of language
Credit: Adapted from Halliday and Matthiessen (2004)

In Chapter 1, we used this model to illustrate our view of language. Each ring represents a component of language, nested together in concentric circles to illustrate the following: As we use language, we make choices simultaneously at the level of context, text, sentence, and word. This model also works to explain how we read: Simultaneously integrating words, sentences, paragraphs, and whole texts, all in the context of the social purpose of the text and its position in the larger context of the world. Successful reading (comprehension) of a text depends on us mastering each ring. If we get tripped up on one ring, our comprehension falls apart. We often think of this happening at the innermost circle, the word, but breakdowns can occur at any of the rings.

> In Lily Wong Fillmore's work with multilingual high school readers, she found that students could read all the words and sentences but still were not able to make logical meaning of the text as a whole. Where they were getting stuck was at the paragraph level. They didn't understand how the sentences were connected inside a paragraph to create larger chunks of meaning and furthermore, how paragraphs are connected to create cohesive whole texts (see for example, Wong Fillmore, 2009).

Most approaches to reading instruction do not take into consideration the importance of integrating these components of language. For example, the whole language approach that begun in the 1980s addressed only the

Purpose

This chapter aims to support you in promoting equitable academic achievement by showing you how you can teach disciplinary reading with the language lens you've been reading about throughout this book. We address the factors described above first by showing you how to address the problem of participation with a strategic interaction move called the "prepare move." Second, we show you how to teach reading in a way that integrates the language components using an approach based on David Rose's 'Reading to Learn' approach.

outer ring, *context and genre*; so-called balanced approaches address the rings one at a time in different parts of the language arts programs; and phonics approaches address only the *word* ring (Rose, 2023). Instead, we need to approach reading instruction in the same way we approach reading, by integrating the components of language. Fragmenting reading into individual components has put large numbers of students at a disadvantage.

What Is Teaching Reading with a Language Lens? Or What Is a Language-Based Approach to Teaching Reading?

Sharon: What is the main point of this section (Table 5.1)?
Anna: Immigration?
Sharon: Great, let's look at this text more closely, what do you think lost in the mists of time means?
Anna: They got lost when they were coming here?
Sharon: Ok, now who is 'they' here?
Anna: I don't know, it doesn't say.
Sharon: Here it says As you learned in Chapter 1. What were you supposed to have learned in Chapter 1?
Anna: I don't remember, I don't think we read that chapter.

The vignette above represents a pivotal moment in our journey to understand what it means to teach reading with a language lens. As part of our research on literacy development for long-term English-learners, we

Table 5.1 Excerpt from an 8th Grade US History Text

Coming to America

The very first American immigrants are lost in the mists of time. Thousands of years ago, they crossed a narrow strip of land that at that time joined northeastern Asia and North America. Their descendants became known as the American Indians.

As you learned in Chapter 1, the next group of immigrants came from Spanish-held Mexico and arrived in what is now southwestern United States in the late 1500s …[2]

administered the reading inventory you just read through. We read the text aloud to Anna (an 8th grader who was born in the United States to multilingual parents) and then asked a series of questions. We were not surprised that Anna missed the question about the metaphor, *lost in time,* but the fact that Anna didn't know who *they* was meant she missed the main point of the first paragraph. We were really surprised that Anna couldn't answer the question about, as you learned in Chapter 1. The answer was right in the text! (the next group of immigrants ...1500s). Why didn't Anna just look there?

We had designed these particular questions from the work of Lily Wong Fillmore and Charles Fillmore's work on Ideal Readers (1983, 2013). The basic premise of this work is that texts are written for a certain type of reader, an "Ideal Reader," who knows exactly what to expect from the text. Here is what the Ideal Reader would know about this particular 8th grade history text:

1. Social studies textbooks often use metaphors like "lost in the mists of time" to present ideas in descriptive ways and in this case "lost in the mists of time" means that we don't know really what happened;

2. "They" is a pronoun that refers back to the subject of the previous sentence, "the very first American immigrants," so that's who the second sentence is talking about;

3. Textbooks often refer back to previous chapters and make connections between those chapters and the present one. "As you learned in Chapter 1" means that the text is going to tell you next what it was you were supposed to have learned. In this case, "the next group of immigrants came from Spanish-held Mexico and arrived in what is now southwestern United States in the late 1500s". Anna, despite being a clever 8th grader who spoke English and Cantonese, was not the Ideal Reader for this text.

> Readers don't just become ideal by being in school for years, but with intentional and explicit instruction by teachers who understand how texts work.

What would have helped Anna? Let's run through a few approaches to teaching reading in social studies reading you likely know and apply them to this situation:

- *Vocabulary development:* Students need to know what the words mean in order to understand the text. In Anna's case, what words did she not know? *Lost, mists, they?* Anna knew all of these words, just not what they meant together and in the context of the text.
- *Comprehension questioning:* Asking strategic questions, from the literal type to the inferential type, with the assumption that the level of difficulty in answering those questions increases as you move up from the literal to the inferential (see Bloom's Taxonomy). This was one of the reasons Sharon was most puzzled; she had asked literal questions, which were supposed to be easy to answer.
- *Building background knowledge:* Pre-teaching the content that the reading is about before students read the text. Was it that Anna didn't know the content? Did she need to know the content to answer the question?

While these approaches are essential in supporting students with reading in the disciplines, they are not enough. The problem Anna had with the text was not that she didn't know the vocabulary, or couldn't make inferential connections, or didn't have the content knowledge. The problem was Anna hadn't picked up on the ways this particular text was presenting the ideas. If she were an ideal reader she would have known that "As you learned in Chapter 1" meant that the next move the text would make would be to tell you what you actually read about in Chapter 1. You didn't have to remember what happened in Chapter 1, or go back and reread Chapter 1. Why did Anna not know this? Her teacher, Sharon, had been teaching reading with a content lens and not a language lens when what Anna needed at that moment was a language lens.

From a language lens, the phrase used in this text "As you learned in Chapter 1" has two functions. One is to connect directly with the reader, using the word "you" to signify that. Two is as a text connector that signals an organizational pattern in the paragraph. If we were teaching Anna now using our language-lens. Here is what we would do. As you read, notice what is different in the way the teacher sets Anna up for success.

Disciplinary Reading

Teacher: This is an introduction to the chapter we are going to read on immigration. It begins by describing how the first group of immigrants got to America by crossing a land bridge between Asia and North America. Here let me show you that on a map.

The first sentence tells us that we don't really know much about this group of immigrants. I'll read it to you, you follow along. *"The very first American immigrants are lost in the mists of time."* There is a metaphor at the end of the sentence that tells us we don't know what happened to them, what's that metaphor?

Anna: Lost in the mists of time

Teacher: That's right. Now, the next sentence tells us about how they crossed the land bridge and where that was. I'll read it: *"Thousands of years ago, they crossed a narrow strip of land that at that time joined northeastern Asia and North America."* Who is "they" referring back to?

Anna: The immigrants, the very first American immigrants.

Teacher: Right. This next sentence is also about the very first American immigrants and it tells us that these people's children, grandchildren, great-grandchildren are related to some native Americans who are still alive today. I'll read that. *"Their descendants became known as the American Indians."* What is the word here that means grandchildren, great-grandchildren?

Anna: Descendants

Teacher: Yep. Now the job of this next paragraph is to remind you of some content that was in Chapter 1 that is related to what you are going to read next. Textbooks do this, they refer back to previous parts of the book. They may say things like "As read in Chapter 1" then they will summarize what you read. Here I'll show you: *"As you learned in Chapter 1, the next group of immigrants came from Spanish-held Mexico and arrived in what is now southwestern United States in the late 1500s."* Instead of "As you read" the text says something similar.

148

Disciplinary Reading

> *Anna:* As you learned
> *Teacher:* That's right, and then after it says as you learned, it tells you what that was supposed to be.
> *Anna:* It says, "the next group of immigrants came from Spanish-held Mexico and arrived in what is now southwestern United States in the late 1500s."
> *Teacher:* That's right. Do you remember reading that in Chapter 1?
> *Anna:* No
> *Teacher:* That's ok, because it doesn't matter, the text just told you what you needed to remember.
> *Anna:* Ok, about the immigrants that came from Mexico.

The moves the teacher used here scaffolded Anna's participation and, as a result, her learning. In this next section, we will discuss the *what, how,* and *why* behind the decisions the teacher made. The aim here is to show you how to address Factor 1 in our problem statement above.

Why Do Many Students Struggle to Read Complex Academic Text?

Factor 1: Lack of student participation and engagement in reading instruction caused by systemic racism in education.

Preparing Students to Participate in Structured Conversations about Text

Let's begin with an excerpt of a primary source document used in the C3 Inquiry on Imperialism for 10th graders.[3] The main inquiry question for this unit is "Do the Boxers deserve a bad rap?" This text is from a recount by Fei Ch'i-hao who was a Chinese Christian. In this text, he recounts the activities of the "Boxers" in the Boxer Rebellion of 1900. Here he describes how Yu Hsien promoted the Boxer Rebellion in Shansi (Table 5.2).

Disciplinary Reading

Table 5.2 Excerpt from *Fei Ch'i-hao: The Boxer Rebellion, 1900*

The wicked Governor, Yü Hsien, scattered proclamations broadcast. These stated that the foreign religions overthrew morality and inflamed men to do evil, so now gods and men were stirred up against them, and Heaven's legions had been sent to exterminate the foreign devils. Moreover, there were the Boxers, faithful to their sovereign, loyal to their country, determined to unite in wiping out the foreign religion. He also offered a reward to all who killed foreigners; either titles, office, or money. When the highest official in the province took such a stand in favor of the Boxers, what could inferior officials do? People and officials bowed to his will, and all who enlisted as Boxers were in high favor. It was a time of license and anarchy when not only Christians were killed but hundreds of others against whom individual Boxers had a grudge.

Now imagine leading a discussion on this text with a group of students for whom such a text would be difficult for them to comprehend by themselves. Assume that by this point in the Inquiry, students have already studied about how the Opium Wars created foreign influence in China and about the Christian missions that were in China at the time. They have been introduced to the Boxers and discussed why the Boxers objected to the foreign missionaries. The purpose of this text is to teach students about what happened during the Boxer Rebellion (Table 5.3).

Table 5.3 The Quizmaster

	Speaker	Dialogue	What's going on?
1	Teacher	Ok, are you guys finished reading?	Asks a question.
2	Some students	Nod	Some, but not all respond
3	Teacher	Let's go over this. Who was Yü Hsien? [The teacher calls on Calvin who had his hand raised].	Asks a question to check understanding.
4	Calvin	He was the one behind the Boxers; he had permission from the Empress to promote all the killing of the foreigners.	Answers the question, uses prior knowledge not in the text.

(Continued)

Table 5.3 (Continued)

	Speaker	Dialogue	What's going on?
5	Teacher	That's right, now what does this text say about what he did?	Tries to redirect students to the content of the text.
6		[The usual students have their hands up]	
7	Teacher	[calls on Destiny, who always has her hand raised] Destiny?	Elicits response from a different student.
8	Destiny	He gave people a reward.	Answers the question using the text, but it is not the answer that the teacher is looking for.
9	Teacher	That's right, but what did he do first?	Asks another question trying to get students to say something like *the first thing he did was issue a proclamation*.
10		[Calvin is the only one with his hand up]	
11	Teacher	Calvin?	Calls on Calvin
12	Calvin	He got support from the Empress.	Tries to guess what is in the teacher's head. Responds accurately, but it's not what the teacher is looking for.
13	Teacher	Yes, but that's not what this text is about. Come on guys, it's right in the text.	Gets frustrated, students are not getting the right answer.
14		[No one has their hand up]	Wait time.
15	Teacher	OK, let me show you. It's in the first sentence. It says that he scattered proclamations. This was really important. What did those proclamations say? Destiny?	Explicitly directs students' attention to the text. Explains why that piece of content is important. Asks the next question. Calls on a student who had previously responded.

Disciplinary Reading

This is not an example of particularly poor teaching, but neither is it an example of a teacher productively making visible how the language of the text works to express the content. We might call this kind of dialogue, "Guess what's in the teacher's head" because the goal of the questioning seemed to be to provide the right answer to the question, What did he do? (Line 5). This right answer, according to what was in the teacher's head, was not "give people rewards" (Destiny's response in Line 8), though accurate according to the text, but "scatter proclamations". No one was able to come up with this answer, so the teacher finally told them what they were looking for (Line 15). Jed Hopkins, a teacher educator and applied linguist, has labeled this type of classroom dialogue where the teacher knows the answer and calls on students to give them the answer the teacher is looking for as the "Quizmaster Dynamic"(Hopkins, 2017).

Here is how we could graphically represent the Quizmaster Dynamic. See Figure 5.2.

When a teacher acts as Quizmaster there are benefits, namely that the teacher has control over both the content and the class, so it serves as an efficient classroom management tool, and it is a very common practice in American schools. However, we need to wonder: What kind of students does this approach benefit? It certainly benefits the students who know the answer and want to please the teacher by letting them know they know the answer. However, how does this approach benefit students who don't get called on? One way a silent student could benefit is by listening to their classmate's responses and learning from them. We all know how unlikely

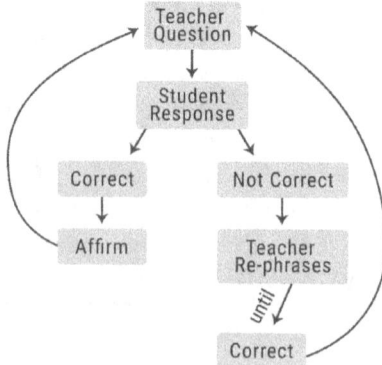

Figure 5.2 The Quizmaster Dynamic

that is. Or the anticipation of being called on might motivate students to prepare, thus learning the material as was intended. Now think about race and gender and English language proficiency, and the students slumped in the back of your classroom with their hoods pulled over their eyes. How does that play into who gets called on and who doesn't? We've met a lot of well-meaning white teachers who were afraid to call on the multilingual learners because they didn't think they would be able to answer the question and didn't want to embarrass them.

Because of these concerns, or simply in efforts to move away from teacher-centered classrooms, a lot of teachers favor student-led discussions. Here is the Quizmaster dialogue from above, this time reimagined as a student-led discussion. See Table 5.4 This time, you can analyze the interaction moves by filling in the "What's going on?" column. See the Chapter 5 Answer Key if needed (Table 5.4).

Table 5.4 Student-Led Discussion

	Speaker	Dialogue	What's going on?
1	Teacher	OK, you are going to discuss this text in your small groups. Focus on Yü Hsien, what he did and why you think he was important.	
2	Calvin	He was the one behind the Boxers; he had permission from the Empress to promote all the killing of the foreigners.	
3	Destiny	He gave people a reward.	
4	Jada	Really? That's so messed up.	
5	Destiny	I know, right.	
6	Calvin	We should talk about why he was important. What do you guys think?	
7	Darius and Jada	[no response, blank looks, seems like they didn't read the text]	
8	Destiny	Well, I think he was important because he was so powerful, I mean he got an entire group of people to hate the foreigners and to want to kill them.	
9	Calvin	Yeah, it's amazing they listened to him.	
10	Teacher	Ok, let's all come back and share.	

If the goal is to reduce teacher-talk, promote students' voices, and provide opportunities for students to make connections to their own lives, student-led discussions serve an important role. However, these discussions don't typically deepen students' understanding of the linguistic resources the text employs to express meaning. Furthermore, who does this type of discussion serve? Who benefited from this discussion? Who didn't? And, a further thing to think about, what were the prerequisites for participation?

It seemed that the students who benefited the most were Destiny and Darius who had clearly connected with the text and seemed to be building on each other's conversation. But what about the ones who didn't speak at all or the ones who hadn't prepared. What about Jada and Darius? This kind of discussion has the potential to be quite valuable in meeting the goal of students connecting content to their lives and supporting each other. But not it doesn't always work for all.

Student-led discussions are an important part of learning content, but they are not enough to support students in learning how content is expressed through language in complex texts. For that students need teachers to make this visible to them using structured conversations around texts. What does this look like? How can we prepare our students to attend to the language in the texts? For those of us who have abandoned the Quizmaster Dynamic in favor of student-led discussions, it looks like a lot more explicit teacher talk than a lot of us are comfortable with, but having structured conversations about language in the context of complex texts is critically important in promoting equitable achievement. Let's look at a revised version of the Quizmaster script (Table 5.5). As you review this, note the differences between it and the original (Table 5.3).

What's different between the original Quizmaster Dynamic in Table 5.3 and Figure 5.2 and this one here in Table 5.5? Both classroom conversations are teacher-led discussions around the text, but the second one has greater equity in who participates and more explicit teaching around how the content is realized through the language of the text.

Let's start by looking more closely at the moves the teacher makes in Line 1. The teacher summarizes the previous paragraph, then paraphrases the first sentence in the focus paragraph, then reads the focal sentence. David Rose (see for example, Rose, 2010; Rose & Martin, 2012), an applied education linguist whose career has focused on promoting equity through literacy pedagogy, has called these kinds of moves "Prepare Moves." The

Table 5.5 Quizmaster Revised

	Speaker	Dialogue	What's going on?
1	Teacher	Let's go over this. As you read in the previous paragraph, Yü Hsien was the one who spearheaded the Boxer Rebellion. This paragraph is going to tell us about how he got support for the Boxers. The first sentence starts by telling us that he put out proclamations that he broadcast all over the place. Follow along while I read the first sentence. *The wicked Governor, Yü Hsien, scattered proclamations broadcast.* What word tells us that the proclamations went everywhere. Jada?	Summarizes the previous paragraph. Paraphrases the first sentence. Reads the first sentence. Focus Question. Cold calls on Jada.
2	Jada	Scattered	Looks at the text, responds.
3	Teacher	That's right, let's imagine what that would look like. Who can act out scattering proclamations. Darius?	Affirms. Invites Darius to act out the sentence.
4		[Darius stands up, and with a grin, throws a bunch of papers in the air]	
5	Teacher	Excellent Darius. Now why is this word *scatter* so important?	Affirms. Focus question for Darius
6	Darius	Well, I am imagining that the guy had all these papers printed with the proclamations and he wanted them everywhere. Like if it said he gave out the proclamations, that would be different, it would mean that it was organized and only a few people got them. Scattered means they were everywhere, like these papers here [gestures to the floor, now a mess with papers].	Responds and elaborates make connections to his life.

(Continued)

Disciplinary Reading

Table 5.5 (Continued)

	Speaker	Dialogue	What's going on?
7	Teacher	[laughing] That's right! Now let's look at the second sentence. This one tells us what the proclamations said.	Affirms. Paraphrases the second sentence.
		Everyone follow along while I read the second sentence: *These stated that the foreign religions overthrew morality and inflamed men to do evil, so now gods and men were stirred up against them, and Heaven's legions had been sent to exterminate the foreign devils.*	Reads the sentence aloud.
		OK, first, what does the word *these* refer to? Destiny?	Focus question. Cold calls on Destiny.
8	Destiny	Proclamations	Looks at text, responds.
9	Teacher	That's right. Everyone draw an arrow from *these* back to proclamations.	Draws everyone's attention to the pronoun referencing in the text.
		Proclamations are directives.	Elaborate.
		Now, what was one thing the proclamations said? Anthony?	Focus question. Cold calls on Anthony.
	Anthony	It says *foreign religions overthrew morality.*	Looks at text, responds.
10	Teacher	That's right. Ok, everyone circle *proclamations* from the first sentence and underline *foreign religions overthrew morality,* and let's draw an arrow between them. Ok, that's one thing the proclamations said, what's another? Olivia?	Draws everyone's attention to how the ideas are being expressed in the text. Focus question. Cold calls on Olivia.
11	continues …		

Disciplinary Reading

summarizing, paraphrasing, and reading of the sentence focus the students on the text and prepare them for the focus question. The focus question has additional "prepare" elements in it: What word tells us that the proclamations *went everywhere*? The italicized phrases prepare the student to look for a word in the sentence that means "went everywhere." The teacher could have asked the students what "scattered" means, but by giving a meaning and asking the students to find a representation of that meaning in the text, the teacher is essentially making explicit how ideas are represented in language, and students are making the connections themselves.

The "prepare" moves promote equitable participation because the entry point to participation is simply paying attention and following along. Note that the teacher cold-called on the students and all were able to respond to the questions.

Here is how we could graphically represent the "prepare" move in the context of the structured conversation above (Figure 5.3).

In this diagram Figure 5.3, each part of the spiral represents a small learning task, for example, unpacking a chunk of ideational meaning within a sentence. The teacher repeats the moves: Prepare, Focus, Affirm, Elaborate for each task.

We have experimented with "prepare moves" in the context of structured discussions around academic texts in our own teaching and research. In one particular research collaboration, we were working with a fourth-grade teacher with the aim of improving her writing workshop curriculum so that it provided better support for multilingual learners (Westerlund & Besser, 2021). Our teacher had three multilingual learners in her class whom she said she didn't call on in front of the class because she didn't want to embarrass them. Sharon led a discussion about a text where she used the "prepare" move. She then called on Henry (one of the multilingual learners) and asked him the question. At first, the class seemed to freeze, and then Henry clearly

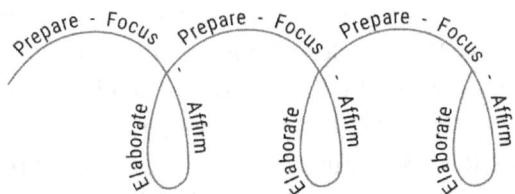

Figure 5.3 Teacher moves to promote equitable participation

and correctly answered the question. This was a pivotal moment for him and also for his teacher who had no idea that he could answer a question like that. So who is the "prepare move" for? Everyone except the privileged high-achieving students. It is true, they do not need the "prepare move" (unless the text is really complex and difficult, even for them).

This "prepare move" can be thought of literally as a move in a participation structure and philosophically as in a way to be explicit in our teaching. It's a technique that scaffolds participation and promotes a culture of belonging, as all students are expected and supported in their participation.

We've shared these dialogues and stories of participation structures to challenge you to rethink your views on explicit teaching and teacher talk. While we strongly advocate for student voices in the classroom, there are times when short bursts of explicit teaching are the most supportive and efficient way we can teach students the language they need to serve the content we want them to learn.

We now move on to the next part of the chapter where we address the second factor in our problem statement:

> # Why Do Many Students Struggle to Read Complex Academic Text?
>
> Factor 2: Approaches to teaching reading that fragment the components of the reading

Integrated Approaches to Teaching Disciplinary Reading

This section focuses on the **how** part of supporting students in reading complex academic texts. We will describe four approaches: Evoking the Story, Detailed Reading, Joint Re-Writing, and Independent Writing. These are based on an approach called Reading to Learn developed by David Rose (see for example, Rose & Martin, 2015) and widespread by his followers, including Andre Ramirez who works with Spanish speakers (e.g., Ramírez, 2023; Ramirez et al., 2021) (Table 5.6).

Disciplinary Reading

Table 5.6 Integrated Approaches to Supporting Academic Reading

Evoking the Story	Detailed Reading	Joint Re-Writing	Independent Re-Writing
Goals: Prepare students for reading the text by making visible the Context of Genre as well as the text and paragraph levels	Goal: Support reading comprehension by making visible the detailed meaning and structure of patterns within sentences	Goal: Support students' integration of genre sentence patterns and words through rewriting the paragraph from the Detailed Reading	Goal: Students integrate for themselves the genre, text and paragraphs, sentence and word groups, and words as they rewrite the paragraph

In your classroom, Evoking the Story could be done in isolation at the Supported Reading Stage of the TLC-DG, or it could be done as part of a mini-TLC-DG cycle that includes the other three. You will see how this would work below. First, though, we illustrate how these approaches combine to create an integrated approach. Consider the Figure 5.4.

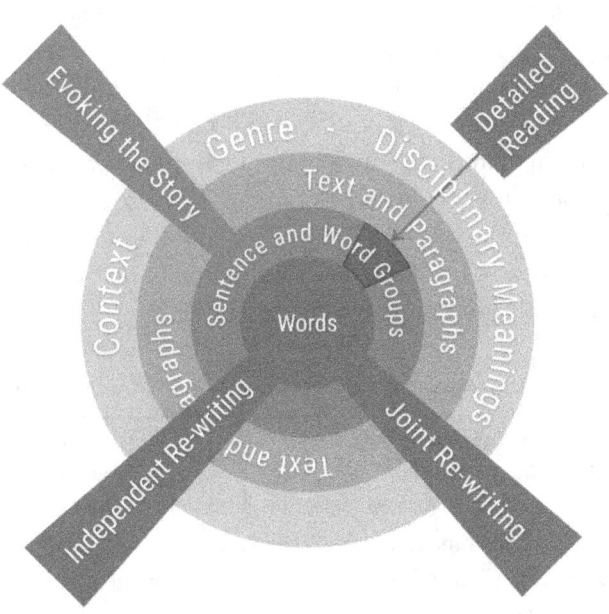

Figure 5.4 Integrated approaches to disciplinary reading

In this diagram, the four approaches are overlaid on our Stratified Model of Language.

- Evoking the Story supports students with the outer two rings, *Context-Genre* and *Text and Paragraph*.
- Detailed Reading supports students with the *Sentence and Word Group* ring.
- Joint Re-Writing (which is similar to Joint Construction from the TLC) integrates support across all rings.
- Independent Writing (which is similar to the stage of this same name on the TLC) integrates support across all rings.

We will describe these approaches in the context of an inquiry and one particular published text, which we refer to as our anchor text, so you can see how to design curriculum to support readers using one text.

The Compelling Question and Anchor Text for This Chapter

The inquiry is from the C3 Framework. Tenth graders read this article as part of the inquiry, "Imperialism."[4] In this inquiry, students explore imperialism in China during the late nineteenth and early twentieth centuries through multifaceted lenses. Here is the supporting question and formative task students do based on the readings we will focus on in this chapter (Table 5.7).

The anchor text is the Featured Source, "The Opium War and Foreign Encroachment". The whole text is reprinted in full in the Appendix. If you have time, go ahead and skim through the whole text now to get a gist; otherwise, read this first paragraph here (Table 5.8).

Table 5.7 Supporting Question 1 from the C3 Inquiry 10th Grade: Imperialism

Supporting Question 1: How did the Opium Wars create foreign influence in China and how did China react?
Formative task: Write 2–3 sentences describing how the Opium Wars created foreign influences in China and the Chinese reactions.
Featured Source: Excerpt from "The Opium War and Foreign Encroachment" (Asia for Educators).

(https://c3teachers.org/inquiries/imperialism/)

Table 5.8 Excerpt from Anchor Text: The Opium War and Foreign Encroachment (Asia for Educators)

"The Opium War and Foreign Encroachment."
Two things happened in the eighteenth century that made it difficult for England to balance its trade with the East. First, the British became a nation of tea drinkers and the demand for Chinese tea rose astronomically. It is estimated that the average London worker spent five percent of his or her total household budget on tea. Second, northern Chinese merchants began to ship Chinese cotton from the interior to the south to compete with the Indian cotton that Britain had used to help pay for its tea consumption habits. To prevent a trade imbalance, the British tried to sell more of their own products to China, but there was not much demand for heavy woolen fabrics in a country accustomed to either cotton padding or silk.

Evoking the Story

The first approach is called Evoking the Story. This is a piece of curriculum from Jed Hopkins' work as inspired by Reading to Learn (Hopkins, 2017). This is a high-leverage approach to scaffolding for comprehension that draws students' attention to the way the content is expressed through the genre structure of the text. If you are just going to do one quick thing that will make a huge difference in your students being able to access and comprehend the text, this would be it. The idea behind Evoking the Story is to prepare students to comprehend a text by evoking the essence of the genre of the text. At first, students will be unfamiliar with the way genres are structured. They won't know what an explanation does or how to identify a claim an author is making. They need you to make visible the generic structure of the text, including the different functions or jobs each phase has. This lack of understanding will manifest in a comprehension problem. Evoking the Story (or text) supports students' understanding of the genre structure of the text.

If you are familiar with Book Talks, where the teacher previews a text by showing students the pictures and telling them briefly what the book will be about, then this will feel similar. Evoking the Story is a scaffolding technique designed to both prepare students to read the text by giving them hints to what each paragraph is about and to engage students in the text, like a good movie trailer does.

Disciplinary Reading

> The important components of Evoking a Story that support readers are as follows:
>
> - Makes visible the genre structure of the text
> - Prepares readers to be Ideal Readers by teaching them what to expect from the text from the text and writer's perspective
> - Promotes the ability to generalize across texts, for example, if I read another explanation, here is what I can expect

Step 1: Ask: What's the Point of This Reading?

You'll want to begin preparation for Evoking a Story by asking yourself a series of questions.

- Why am I assigning this text? [So students can learn the content they need to write about for their formative assessment on how the Opium Wars created foreign influences in China and the Chinese reactions.]
- What question from my inquiry does this text have the content for the students to answer? [How did the Opium Wars create foreign influence in China and how did China react?]
- What discussions do I want my students to have as a result of reading this text? [What was the trade imbalance and how did that lead to foreign powers influencing China, etc.]
- What is the content I want my students to understand? [The trade imbalance, the various events and reactions that led to Opium Wars, the foreign presence in China, etc.]

You'll use the answers to these questions to explain the purpose for the students; see Table 5.10.

Step 2: Paraphrase the Text

Next, you would paraphrase the text paragraph by paragraph. We like to do this in table form. As you are paraphrasing, also think about the job each paragraph is doing and how it supports the whole. This will get you to think about genre.

Disciplinary Reading

Table 5.9 Paraphrasing the Anchor Text

Paraphrased text	Original text
It's the end of the eighteenth century. British people wanted Chinese tea, so Britain sold cotton they got from India to pay for the tea.	Two things happened in the eighteenth century that made it difficult for England to balance its trade with the East. First, the British became a nation of tea drinkers and the demand for Chinese tea rose astronomically. It is estimated that the average London worker spent five percent of his or her total household budget on tea. Second, northern Chinese merchants began to ship Chinese cotton from the interior to the south to compete with the Indian cotton that Britain had used to help pay for its tea consumption habits. To prevent a trade imbalance, the British tried to sell more of their own products to China, but there was not much demand for heavy woolen fabrics in a country accustomed to either cotton padding or silk.
But it turned out that China grew its own cotton, and didn't want it from Britain. So Britain had to find something else to sell. They tried wool, they had a lot of sheep making wool in Britain, but China didn't want British wool, they preferred silk and cotton for their clothes.	
Continue: Paraphrasing for paragraph 2 See Appendix, Table 5.18	Continue: Original text, paragraph 3

Here is what we would do for the first paragraph. The entire text with the paraphrasing is in the Appendix at the end of this chapter (Table 5.9).

After paraphrasing the text, you could use this to introduce the text to your students before they read the text. You would prepare them to read the text independently (or in groups) by telling them why they are reading the text, and what the text is about, highlighting what is important about the text, telling them about the content of the text, and most importantly how it connects to the inquiry. The word evoke is intentional here. The idea here is to evoke students' interest in the content and prepare them for their own reading, but not to give everything away. Try to build tension and suspense. You'll also invite students to annotate their texts for the purpose of scaffolding their independent reading (Table 5.10).

This would go a long way toward supporting students' independent reading of the text, as you will have prepared them to pay attention to the pertinent content. In fact, this entire script is a "prepare move."

Disciplinary Reading

Table 5.10 Evoking the Story Content Focus

Name the purpose for the students	Tell the students that the purpose of reading this text is to learn the content to answer the question "How did the Opium Wars create foreign influence in China and how did China react?" Tell them they will use this content for the formative assessment assignment in which they write a paragraph answering that question.
Overall text content preview	Summarize the text in a few sentences. You would say, for example: *This text is about imperialism and how that impacted China. It explains how the Opium Wars started and how foreigners got so involved in China.*
Make connections to previous learning to activate background knowledge	Make connections to previous content learned as applicable: *Let's remind ourselves about trade imbalances and what that means, that concept is really important in this text. Remember the activity we did where we acted out trade imbalances. Some of you had pencils with no erasers that you were trying to trade for sticks of gum. How did that work out?*
Explain task	Explain to the students that you are going to go quickly through the text, giving a preview of each paragraph which will help them focus their reading, but they won't be reading the text right now. Instead, they will be making notes in the margins.
Paragraph 1 Preview	Summarize the paragraph in a few sentences and leave room for the students to discover what happens through their own reading. Use the paraphrasing you did as preparation, but make sure not to give everything away. You could say, for example: *This first paragraph tells us how the trade imbalance first began. The British people wanted Chinese tea, and they had to figure out something to trade with China to pay for the tea. Britain had a bunch of cotton from India so they used that. But something happens so Britain has to find something else to trade.*
Teaser	
Student note-taking	(Note-taking) You invite students to jot a few notes, or a key question on their text to help them focus their reading, for example: *Everyone, write this question in the margin: What happened that made it so Britain couldn't trade cotton anymore? Then, when you read later, you'll be answering this question.*
Continue with the remaining paragraphs (see the Appendix for a complete version of this Evoking the Story script).	

Disciplinary Reading

However, you have another opportunity here and that is to make the genre of the text visible to the students so they can gain a deeper understanding of how disciplinary texts work and be able to generalize this knowledge with other texts they will encounter in social studies.

Step 3: Identify the Genre and Backward Outline the Text

What is the genre of this text? Is it an argument, an explanation, or a narrative? Some of the above, all of the above? It is not always clear what genre the text is. There are lots of hybrid mash-up genres out there. But, as you'll recall, genres exist to serve purposes, so begin with purpose. The purpose of this text is to describe what happened. The text begins with "Two things happened...," then goes on to tell us about the first event and then the second event. Does this text feel like an argument or an explanation? We think of explanation as it describes events for the purpose of explaining the events leading to the Opium Wars and how foreign encroachment happened. The text is not making claims and supporting them with evidence like an argument would do. What kind of explanation is it? We think it's a factorial explanation that has the purposes of identifying and describing a multitude of factors that led to an event/situation. The job of *The Opium War and Foreign Encroachment is* to name and describe the factors that led to the Opium Wars and also the foreign encroachment on Chinese soil. This is why this text was chosen to support the inquiry. This particular text describes these factors as a series of problems, solutions, and reactions to those solutions. These all occurred over a period of time. So the framework of our outline would look something like this, see Figure 5.5.

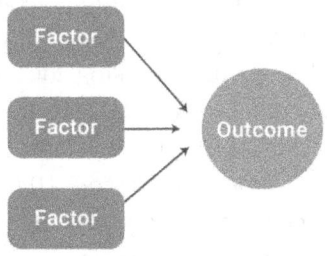

Figure 5.5 Factorial explanation

Disciplinary Reading

This particular text, like many your students read, does not clearly identify the factors. These are expressed through the content of the text. Most of your students will need you to pull these out for them. So, the next part of your preparation would be to backward design an outline that identifies these factors and illuminates the series of problems, solutions, and reactions that describe each factor. Here is how we have interpreted these from this text.

An outline or table like Table 5.11 would be useful in itself as a tool to make the genre visible to the students. The important concept here is that the disciplinary concept of factors leading to an outcome is expressed through the genre structures like the ones in this explanation. You might use this table to build out with students or have advanced students complete themselves (with a blank or semi-completed version). Additionally, with this in your back pocket, you can add another layer to the scaffolding you did by Evoking the Story with the paraphrasing by explicitly drawing students' attention to how the factors are expressed with language in the text.

Step 4: Map the Genre Stages to the Text

Here is the table where we paraphrased the text, but this time we have added in the genre stages to illustrate how the Factors as realized through problems, solutions, and reactions are expressed in the text. Note that we have underlined Factor 1 both in the Genre Structure column and then in the text where we would show students how Factor 1 is expressed in the text.

Step 5: Add a Focus on Genre Stages to Your Evoking the Story Script

Table 5.12 could be used as a preparation tool for yourself or something that you could build out with your students. As a preparation tool, it supports the following expanded version of Evoking the Story, where you make explicit not just how the content is expressed but how the genre structure is realized through the text. Table 5.13 illustrates how you might do this. We have left in parts of the script from Table 5.10 (these are highlighted) to illustrate how you could combine both scripts to meet two objectives, one to prepare students for the content of the text (from Table 5.10) as well as to prepare students for the genre of the text.

Table 5.11 Genre Structure: Multiple Factors, Problems, and Reactions Leading to One Outcome

What factors led to the Opium Wars and foreign encroachment in China?			
Factor 1: Trade Imbalance that started with a problem and attempts to solve the problem	**Factor 2:** Opium Public Health Problem that led to an unresolvable conflict between Britain and China (the first Opium War)	**Factor 3:** Chinese defeat in the Opium War provides an opening for foreigners to come in and do business and missionary work	**Outcome:** China becomes politically weak, and colonized by western nations (Britain, Russia, France)
Problem: Britain wanted Chinese tea, but didn't have anything to trade for it that China wanted	**Problem:** Chinese people buy opium from the British. Large numbers get addicted	**Problem:** China is defeated. There are a series of "unequal treaties" that disadvantage China	
Solution: Britain tries cotton, then wool, then finally opium	**Solution:** Chinese government tries to stop the epidemic by cracking down on the sale of opium, but sales continue	**Solution:** China fights back, and there is another war, China loses again, and then rebels with the Boxer Rebellion	
Reactions: China rejects cotton, wool, but accepts opium (at least on the Black Market)	**Reactions:** China Confiscates foreign supplies of opium, and forces foreign merchants to agree not to sell opium to China or they would be punished by Chinese law	**Reactions:** Foreigners (and not just British) keep encroaching and colonizing China	

Disciplinary Reading

Table 5.12 Genre Stages Mapped with Text

	Paraphrased text	Original text	Genre stages
1	It's the end of the eighteenth century. British people wanted Chinese tea, so Britain sold cotton they got from India to pay for the tea. But it turned out that China grew its own cotton, and didn't want it from Britain. So Britain had to find something else to sell. They tried wool, they had a lot of sheep making wool in Britain, but China didn't want British wool, they preferred silk and cotton for their clothes.	Two things happened in the eighteenth century that made it <u>difficult for England to balance its trade with the East</u>. First, the British became a nation of tea drinkers and the demand for Chinese tea rose astronomically. It is estimated that the average London worker spent five percent of his or her total household budget on tea. Second, northern Chinese merchants began to ship Chinese cotton from the interior to the south to compete with the Indian cotton that Britain had used to help pay for its tea consumption habits. To prevent a trade imbalance, the British tried to sell more of their own products to China, but there was not much demand for heavy woolen fabrics in a country accustomed to either cotton padding or silk.	<u>Factor 1</u> Trade Imbalance that started with a problem and attempts to solve the problem **Problem:** Britain wanted Chinese tea, but didn't have anything to trade for it that China wanted **Solution:** Britain tries cotton, then wool **Reactions:** China rejects cotton, wool

See Appendix for the complete table.

Disciplinary Reading

Table 5.13 Evoking the Story with Genre Stages

Name the genre and connect to purpose of reading	You'll say something like: *This text is an explanation. It is going to explain to you how the Opium Wars created foreign influence in China and how China reacted. It is going to give you the content you need to write your formative assessment.* *This text is not just any old explanation, but a factorial one, which means it will tell you the factors that led to this foreign influence.* [You could show them a diagram of a factorial explanation.] *This text is interesting in that it describes the factors as a series of problems and solutions. I'll show you what I mean.*
Explain what the students need to do	*Everyone needs a copy of the text, a highlighter and a pen or pencil. We are going to preview the text, but not read it just yet. I'll tell you what to highlight, and I'll guide you in making some notes so that when you read the text on your own, you'll be able to identify these factors and problems and solutions.* [You can show students how you markup the text using digital tools. You can also create an outline on the whiteboard as you go.]
Overall text content preview Make connections to previous learning to activate background knowledge	Summarize the text in a few sentences. You would say, for example: *This text is about imperialism and how that impacted China. It explains how the Opium Wars started and how foreigners got so involved in China.* Make connections to previous content learned as applicable: *Let's remind ourselves about trade imbalances and what that means, that concept is really important in this text. Remember the activity we did where we acted out trade imbalances. Some of you had pencils with no erasers that you were trying to trade for sticks of gum. How did that work out?*
Make visible Factor 1	Show students how the first factor is expressed in the text. Say something like: *The first factor that explains how the Opium Wars created foreign influence in China was the trade imbalance.* *Look at this first sentence; it says "Two things happened in the eighteenth century that made it difficult for England to balance its trade with the East." This introduces the first factor, which is the trade imbalance.*
Student note-taking	Highlight "difficult for England to balance its trade with the East." Label that Factor 1.

(Continued)

Table 5.13 (Continued)

Paragraph 1 Preview	Summarize the paragraph in a few sentences and leave room for the students to discover what happens through their own reading. Use the paraphrasing you did as preparation, but make sure not to give everything away. You could say, for example: *This first paragraph tells us how the trade imbalance first began. The British people wanted Chinese tea, and they had to figure out something to trade with China to pay for the tea. Britain had a bunch of cotton from India so they used that. But something happens so Britain has to find something else to trade.*
Teaser	
Student note-taking	(Note-taking) You invite students to jot a few notes, or a key question on their text to help them focus their reading, for example: *Everyone, write this question in the margin: What happened that made it so Britain couldn't trade cotton anymore? Then when you read later, you'll be answering this question.*
	Continue working through the preview of the text, pointing out that Factor 2 shows up in paragraph 3, Factor 3 in paragraphs 4–5, and the outcome in paragraph 5, and have students underline and label where these Factors begin. See Tables 5.18 and 5.19 in the Appendix for more guidance.

Summary of Evoking the Story

The purpose of this scaffolding approach to teaching academic reading in social studies is to prepare students for an independent reading of the text. The preparation explicitly draws students' attention to the way the content they need to comprehend is realized in the text, specifically through the genre structure of the text. During Evoking the Story, you would go through the text previewing it for the students and as you do that directing them to annotate the text in strategic ways that will support comprehension. You would make sure not to give the whole text away, but to leave teasers, little clues that the students need to read and find out about. The approach works for any and all genres from arguments to narratives and the hybrid ones in between.

> ## Evoking the Story Steps
>
> **Step 1:** Ask: What's the point of this reading?
> **Step 2:** Paraphrase the text
> **Step 3:** Identify the genre and backward outline the text
> **Step 4:** Map the Genre Structure to the text
> **Step 5:** Add a focus on Genre Structure to your Evoking the Story script

> ## Try it out
>
> Follow the steps above to create an Evoking the Story script for a reading you are assigning your students.

Detailed Reading

Evoking the Story focused on how disciplinary understandings such as factors and outcomes are expressed in a text at the levels of *context and genre* and *text and paragraph* (see Figure 5.4). This next approach to supporting academic reading, Detailed Reading, draws attention to how ideas are expressed in *sentences and word groups* (see Figure 5.4) through building blocks of meanings made with single words and word groups. It is a high-leverage approach that supports all readers with complex text.

How to Analyze Sentences to Identify How Meaning Is Made with Groups of Words

This approach relies on a way of analyzing language to make visible the functional parts of a sentence. Consider the following sentence from our anchor text:

> Northern Chinese merchants began to ship Chinese cotton from the interior to the south.

Disciplinary Reading

In order to comprehend this sentence, your brain went through a rapid-fire series of questions, *What? What's happening? Where?* Let's put that into table form:

What?	What's happening?	What?	Where?
Northern Chinese merchants	began to ship	Chinese cotton	from the interior to the south.

Those questions, which we refer to as Probe Questions, provide the foundation for Detailed Reading as you'll see below. First, though, it is helpful to have some metalanguage to describe what's going on in our sentences. Let's look at this sentence again:

> Northern Chinese merchants/began to ship/Chinese cotton/from the interior to the south.

It's been divided up into word groups, separated by a single slash. It has one verb group, **began to ship,** which makes this a single clause. (Many of the sentences you will find in your texts will have additional clauses with their own verbs. We will address this later.) The verb group is an action verb, and the sentence is telling us about the action that occurred and the people and things involved in that action. We can label the word groups in the following way:

Participant	Process	Participant	Circumstance
Northern Chinese merchants	**began to ship**	Chinese cotton	from the interior to the south.
Noun phrase	Verb phrase	Noun phrase	Prepositional phrase

You'll notice that we have labeled the verb as *Process*, the noun groups as *Participants*, and the prepositional phrase as *Circumstance*. Processes are word groups that are typically realized by verb groups; Participants are word groups that are often realized by noun groups and circumstances are words that are realized by prepositional phrases, adverbs, or clauses containing a prepositional phrase or clause. These terms, Process, Participant, and Circumstance, which we call meaning elements, were developed to help us understand the functional system whereby language allows us to express things as what is happening, to whom, where, when, how, and why. While understanding the names of the parts of speech, like noun and verb, is important, we have found that focusing on the probe questions and functional terms is most useful in supporting reading comprehension as it keeps us focused on what the language is doing. Understanding how groups of words function to create certain types of meaning is a key aspect of making language visible to our students and has a great deal of pedagogical usefulness for supporting students in reading and writing. To make the functions of language visible we need to uncover the type of meaning that is underlying each of these grammatical elements (the groups of words we labeled above). We do this by identifying the probe question underneath the element. For example,

- *Processes* are word groups that address probing questions like "What's happening?" "What's the event?" "How are things related or defined?";
- *Participants* are word groups that address the probing questions "who?" or "what?"; and
- *Circumstances* are word groups that address probing questions like "when?" "where?" "how?" and "why?"

Imagine having a conversation with students around a difficult chunk of text and you help them uncover the meaning by asking these probe questions. You would be supporting them with literal comprehension of the ideas of the text and enabling them to make meaning from the sentence.

Though not all language is going to fit into these categories, Participants, Processes, and Circumstances are the three elements that together are a powerhouse for meaning-making, for expressing ideas (see Figure 1.6 in Chapter 1). In Detailed Reading, we are focusing on the Register Level and the Metafunction we are paying attention to with this kind of analysis is Field, particularly ideational meaning that expresses how ideas are packaged at the phrase and word level inside sentences.

Let's quickly look at a sentence that has more than one Process (and therefore more than one clause). As you know, these types of sentences are very common in social studies explanations and arguments.

Disciplinary Reading

> Each of these defeats/ brought / more foreign demands, greater indemnities // that China had to repay, more foreign presence along the coast, // and /more foreign participation/ in China's political and economic life./

What is this text about?					
What?	What's happening?	What?		What?	What kind?
Each of these defeats	Brought	more foreign demands, greater indemnities// that China had to repay, more foreign presence along the coast,	And	more foreign participation	in China's political and economic life.
Participant	Process	Participant	Conjunction	Participant	Circumstance

As you'll see, we put the conjunction "and" on its own. Conjunctions are important when we are looking at the relationship between ideas, but not as important when we are talking about the ideas themselves expressing meaning. You'll also note that we put the entire clause, *that China had to repay, more foreign presence along the coast* in the box that answered the question "brought what?." Imagine asking your students, "What did the defeats bring?" (Answer: More foreign demands, and indemnities that China had to repay and more foreign presence along the coast). However, in some cases, particularly when the clause contains a lot of content you want to make sure students comprehend, you may want to unpack the clause on its own. See below:

Conjunction	Who?	What's happening?	Implied conjunction	What?	Where?
That	China	had to repay	(and)	more foreign presence	along the coast,
	Participant	Process		Participant	Circumstance

If you unpacked the clause this way, you could ask your students:

- "What's happening here?" (Answer: China had to repay debts because they lost the war.)
- "What else happened because China lost the war?" (Answer: there was more foreign presence.)
- "Where?" (Answer: along the coast.)

Let's summarize. At the sentence level, content is realized through language that expresses three types of meaning:

1. the *who* and *what*
2. the *what's happening*
3. the *where, how, when, why*

We can use the metalanguage: Participant, Process, and Circumstance to label the words and word groups. What is going to be most relevant to you as you support your students with reading comprehension are the prompts that go with these three types of meaning. The following table (Table 5.14) may be helpful.

Now it's your turn. Take this next sentence and analyze it to identify who does what to whom, where, when, and why. Divide the sentence into its meaning elements and put them in the middle row. We have gotten you started (Exercise 5.15):

Here is another sentence to practice (Exercise 5.16).

Table 5.14 Representing Ideational Meaning

Meaning elements	Associated probe question	Sample text
Circumstance	When, where, how, why?	In 1843
Participant	Who? What?	France and the United States, and Russia
Process	What's happening? What's the event? How are things related or defined?	negotiated

Disciplinary Reading

> More ports were open to foreign residents, trade, and foreigners, especially missionaries, were allowed free movement and business anywhere in the country.

What is this sentence about? This time try coming up with the probe questions and put those in the top row.

What if you are not sure which group of words goes where? As you delve into this work, you are going to have lots of questions and wonderings about how to analyze certain sentences. Rest assured, this is a flexible system of analysis designed to support your teaching, so please don't overthink the analyses. Social studies texts are notorious for complex sentences with a lot of clauses. In many cases, clauses will answer the question, *what?*

5.15 Try it out

In 1900, an international army suppressed the anti-foreign Boxer Rebellion in northern China.

When?	What?	What's happening?	What?	Where?
			the anti-foreign Boxer Rebellion	
Circumstance	Participant	Process	Participant	Circumstance

Now that you know something about the transitivity system whereby language enables us to express fundamental meanings as what is happening, to whom, where, when, and how, you are ready to prepare a series of reading lessons we group under the category of Detailed Reading.

Step 1: Select a Paragraph

Detailed Reading is designed to scaffold a small piece of a complex text, one that the majority of your students will need support with. We recommend choosing a paragraph tied to your learning targets. Imagine that for this paragraph the learning target was: *I can explain what a trade balance is and relate that to the Opium Wars.*

> ### 5.16 Try it out
> More ports were open to foreign residence and trade, and
>
> | More ports | Were open to | Foreign residence and trade | Conjunction And |
> |---|---|---|---|
> | Participant | Process | Participant | Conjunction |
>
> foreigners, especially missionaries, were allowed free movement and business anywhere in the country.
>
> | Foreigners | especially missionaries | were allowed | free movement and business | anywhere in the country |
> |---|---|---|---|---|
> | Participant | Circumstance | Process | Participant | Circumstance |

Here is the paragraph. We have numbered the sentences and put the embedded clauses in brackets if helpful:

> 1. Two things happened in the eighteenth century [that made it difficult for England to balance its trade with the East]. 2. First, the British became a nation of tea drinkers and [the demand for Chinese tea rose astronomically]. 3. It is estimated [that the average London worker spent five percent of his or her total household budget on tea]. 4. Second, northern Chinese merchants began to ship Chinese cotton from the interior to the south to compete with the Indian cotton [that Britain had used to help pay for its tea consumption habits]. 5. To prevent a trade imbalance, the British tried to sell [more of their own products to China], but there was [not much demand for heavy woolen fabrics in a country accustomed to either cotton padding or silk].

Disciplinary Reading

Step 2: Analyze the Paragraph, Sentence by Sentence to Identify the Elements of Meaning

There are many ways to analyze the paragraph, sentence by sentence to identify the elements of meaning. You can use tables like the ones above; you can also color-code the text (e.g., red for participants, green for process, blue for circumstances). See the Appendix (Table 5.20) for how we annotated this paragraph using gray scale. You could also write the probe questions right in the text. The goal is to first understand for yourself how the meanings are realized, and then you'll build this preparation into a script.

Here, we invite you to do the analysis on this paragraph to continue to practice and so you can see how we have applied this analysis to our Detailed Reading script below. We have filled in some of the blanks for you. Analyze the clauses (that are in brackets) as one chunk of meaning. Feel free to adjust the question prompts as needed. For example, in Sentence 1, we used the question, "What else?" Instead of just "what?" We have found that "what else?" is a handy Prompt for labeling groups of words that function to add additional information that describes the main Participant. See the Chapter 5 Answer Key as needed (Exercises 5.17–5.21).

5.17 Try it out

Sentence 1: Two things happened in the eighteenth century [that made it difficult for England to balance its trade with the East].

What?	What's happening?	When?	What else?
			That made it difficult for England to balance its trade with the East.
		Circumstance	

Disciplinary Reading

5.18 Try it out

Sentence 2: First, the British became a nation of tea drinkers and the demand for Chinese tea rose astronomically.

		What?	
Text connective			
First	The British		a nation of tea drinkers
Text connective		*Process*	
Conjunction		**What kind?**	**how?**
		for Chinese tea	
		Circumstance	*circumstance*

5.19 Try it out

Sentence 3: It is estimated that the average London worker spent five percent of his or her total household budget on tea.

What?	conjunction	Who	What's happening	How?
is estimated	that			Five percent of his or her total budget
		Participant		

179

Disciplinary Reading

5.20 Try it out

Sentence 4: Second, northern Chinese merchants began to ship Chinese cotton from the interior to the south to compete with the Indian cotton [that Britain had used to help pay for its tea consumption habits].

Text Connective			What?
Second			
Text Connective		Process	
	What's happening?	How?	
From the interior to the south			that Britain has used to help pay for its tea consumption habits

5.21 Try it out

Sentence 5. To prevent a trade imbalance, the British tried to sell [more of their own products to China], but there was [not much demand for heavy woolen fabrics in a country accustomed to either cotton padding or silk].

			What's happening?	what?
To prevent				
	Participant	Participant		
Conjunction	What	How are things related or defined?		what?
But		Was		not much demand for heavy woolen fabrics in a country accustomed to either cotton padding or silk
	Participant			

180

Step 3: Write Yourself a Detailed Reading Script

While you won't always need a script, it's a good idea to do while you are learning this approach. As you will see below, what happens in a Detailed Reading session is the teacher scaffolds a reading of a complex text by providing explicit support by pointing out the wordings creating the elements of meaning and naming language features if appropriate. The teacher uses their prior analysis of the ideational meaning of the text to make decisions on which elements of meaning to draw students' attention to. Additionally, the teacher asks students to highlight chunks of meaning as they go. This highlighting serves two purposes, one it keeps students engaged, and two, students can use the highlighted chunks in a follow-up activity where they use those chunks to reconstruct the text and create a paraphrased summary.

Here is an example of a Detailed Reading script you could use for the first paragraph of *The Opium War and Foreign Encroachment*. This excerpt covers the first three sentences, for the rest of the paragraph see the script in the Appendix. Notice that we have used the discourse moves, Prepare, Focus, Elaborate. The teacher in the script is cold calling on students; note the variety of students that participate. For this script, imagine the students have not seen the text before, so the teacher introduces its purpose in the same way you would for Evoking the Story.

Imagine the students have an unmarked copy of the paragraph in front of them and they have highlighters or pens to use for underlining (Table 5.15).

1. Let's think about what was going on in this script. The teacher drew attention to the way the language in the text expresses three types of meaning: (1) the who and what; (2) the what's happening; and (3) the where, how, when, why. One way this was done was by asking Prompt questions. Example: Line 5: **When** did this begin, Marcus? [in the eighteenth century]. Another way this was achieved was by asking students to find wordings that represent certain meanings. Example: Line 9: **What word** tells us that what happened was a change? Lucy? [became]
2. The teacher prepared students to be successful in identifying the language that expressed the meaning in four ways: (1) Summarizing

Table 5.15 Sample Detailed Reading Script for Paragraph 1 of *The Opium War and Foreign Encroachment*

What the teacher is doing	What the teacher would say
Orientation to the social purpose	1. Imagine all the students have this text in front of them. You've told the students what the social purpose of the text is. *That this is a factorial explanation whose job it is to explain how the trade imbalance between Britain and China came about.*
Paragraph Summary (Prepare)	2. Then, you tell them you are going to have them look at the first paragraph. You tell them something like, *In this paragraph we're going to hear about how the trade imbalance started. British people wanted Chinese tea, so Britain sold Indian cotton to China to pay for the tea. This was balanced, but then China didn't want the cotton Britain was trading for the tea. So Britain had to find something else to sell. They tried wool fabrics, but China didn't want what Britain had to sell (heavy woolen fabrics). So the imbalance was that Britain wanted what China had, but China didn't want anything Britain had to trade.*
Sentence Summary (Prepare) Read aloud	3. You say something like, *The first sentence is a preview that tells us that there are two things that made it difficult for England to balance trade with China.* 4. You read: *Two things happened in the eighteenth century that made it difficult for England to balance its trade with the East.*
Prepare Focus Students underline	5. (Prep) *This sentence tells us when this trade imbalance began.* (Focus) *When did this begin, Marcus?* [in the eighteenth century]. *That's right, let's underline that.*
Sentence Summary (Prepare) Read aloud	6. You say something like *the second sentence tells us about the first factor which is that all of a sudden, most people in Britain started drinking tea, which came from China, and wanted lots and lots of Chinese tea.* 7. You read: *First, the British became a nation of tea drinkers and the demand for Chinese tea rose astronomically.*

(Continued)

Disciplinary Reading

Table 5.15 (Continued)

What the teacher is doing	What the teacher would say

Focus
Students
  underline
Prepare
Focus
Focus
Elaborate?
Prepare
Focus
Elaborate
Students
  underline
	8. (Focus) *Who is this sentence about? Allyson?* [the British] *that's right, let's underline that.*
	9. *The first part of this sentence tells us that the British hadn't always drunk a lot of tea, but that what happened was a change.* (Focus) *What word tells us that what happened was a change? Lucy?* [became]. *That's right.*
	10. (Focus) *the British became what? James?* [a nation of tea drinkers]. *Excellent, go ahead and underline a nation of tea drinkers.* (Do they know about the British culture of drinking tea that still exists today? Maybe elaborate upon this.)
	11. (Prep) *The second part of this sentence tells us that because the British people now wanted to drink a lot of tea, the demand for Chinese tea increased.* (Focus) *What word tells us that the demand rose a lot? Chenita?* [astronomically]. *Right.* (Elaborate) *astronomically means it rose a lot and it rose quickly. Let's underline this whole clause, "the demand rose astronomically."*
	Continue for the rest of the paragraph. See the Appendix for the complete script.

the paragraph; (2) Summarizing the sentence; Reading the sentence aloud; (3) Describing how the sentence is expressing meaning. Example: Line 9. **The first part of this sentence tells us** that the British hadn't always drunk a lot of tea, but that what happened was a change.

3. The teacher used different types of moves: Prepare, Focus, Elaborate, Affirm. We discussed the Prepare move-in #1 here. The Focus move includes the teacher cold calling on a student and asking a question related to one of the probe questions (What, What's Happening, How, Why, When) used to identify the three types of meaning. The Elaborate move is when the teacher took the opportunity to elaborate upon the way language is being

Disciplinary Reading

  used. Though not labeled, the teacher used quick affirmations throughout to build students' confidence and move the conversation along.

4. The students were following along, responding when called on, and underlining and annotating as directed. Notably, the students did not ask questions nor did the teacher invite them. This was intentional to keep the focus on the text and to keep things quickly moving along.

  You may be wondering how long it would take to follow the script and how attentive the students would be. Teachers we work with always wonder the same thing, so we tried out this script (the full paragraph version in the Appendix) with a group of high schoolers, and the answer is that it took a little over ten minutes. As for engagement, it's very high, for several reasons. First, all students have a copy of the text and something to underline or highlight. For each sentence, they have to highlight one or two words (and the accuracy of this is relevant to the next task, which the students know about). Second, there is the cold calling. The teacher cold calls on students, so they have to pay attention. The last reason we think the engagement is high is because the "prepare moves" set students up to successfully answer the questions, and for many of us, getting the right answer and getting affirmed by the teacher feels good and worth engaging in (Table 5.16).

  Essentially what Detailed Reading does is scaffold the process of reading a text in a highly supported way that draws students' attention to how the chunks of meaning are expressed ideationally in the text. Detailed Reading is intense and is meant to be brief, about 10–15 minutes done with a strategic part of the text. The idea is that students learn to generalize and learn how to recognize what was focused on in the Detailed Reading in other parts of the text, so you might do a Detailed Reading of one paragraph of the text and then have students independently or in small groups read the rest. Some of you may push back on the intense focus on literal comprehension. But our goal is to make how texts work visible, so this is incredibly important. As with other ways of scaffolding, at some point, we want the students to be able to internalize the scaffold into a dialogue in their heads and apply it to their own reading, so as they read they are

Table 5.16 Pushing Back on Detailed Reading?

Possible Teacher Push Backs	Benefits of Detailed Reading
It takes too much time!	It actually takes 10–15 minutes.
I don't have time to go through the whole textbook chapter sentence by sentence.	There is no need to work with an entire text. You should select a passage strategically.
Students are going to get bored!	Actually, in our research, student engagement was very high because they experience success with this model. They work with a copy of the text and get to underline and highlight the language in the text. The Prepare moves set up students to answer questions successfully and that gives them a boost to feel good and it feels worth engaging in.
Cold calling on students is unfair!	Cold calling is not unfair. It encourages students to pay attention; however, this model sets them up for success with the Prepare moves.
This focuses too much on literal meanings!	Detailed Reading teaches students how to find meanings in texts; it makes how language works in texts visible.
It's too much scaffolding!	It may seem like that, but without teaching, how will students identify that passive voice hides agency? As with other ways of scaffolding, at some point we want the students to be able to internalize the scaffold into a dialogue in their heads and apply it to their own reading, so as they read they are asking themselves, *who is this about, what's happening, where, how, why, what else?*
My students read just fine on their own!	Detailed Reading is not meant to replace opportunities for students to create inferential meanings from the texts, nor is it meant to be a prerequisite for that important kind of work with texts but as a supplementary activity that temporarily supports the reading of complex texts.
Why would I need to identify parts of speech? I am a social studies teacher, not a language teacher!	You may not realize this, but you are teaching social studies through language. It's hard to see the water in which you swim. Detailed Reading helps you see that water and supports students in seeing how social studies meanings are encoded through nouns, verbs, and prepositional phrases.

Disciplinary Reading

asking themselves, *who is this about, what's happening, where, how, why, what else?* Importantly, Detailed Reading is not meant to replace opportunities for students to create inferential and personal meaning from the texts, nor is it meant to be a prerequisite for that important kind of work with texts, but as a supplementary activity that temporarily supports the reading of complex texts.

Summary of Detailed Reading

The important components of Detailed Reading that support readers are as follows:

- Supports comprehension through a focus on the functions of the components of the sentence
- Promotes internal dialogue that students can generalize to other texts and thus build their skills
- Builds readers confidence

The following table summarizes the steps we outlined above.

> **Step 1:** Select a paragraph.
> **Step 2:** Analyze the paragraph sentence by sentence to identify the elements of meaning.
> **Step 3:** Write yourself a Detailed Reading script.

After doing a Detailed Reading like this with a whole class, there are many things you could do next. For example, students could discuss the content in any number of ways making connections to other texts, videos, and their own lives. Students could continue reading the text independently, perhaps with the Evoking the Story kind of scaffolding as needed. Detailed Reading is excellent for a whole-class activity, but you could also use it for small groups. You could also teach students how to do the analyses you did above in Tables 5.17–5.21. Advanced students could do that work independently.

Two particularly useful follow-up activities and the last two approaches we will show you are Joint Re-Writing Construction from Notes and Independent Writing. If you look back at Figure 5.4, you'll see that these activities integrate all of the components of reading. You may wonder how these activities address the inner circle, word. It is the act of writing the words down and spelling them that addresses this ring of the circle. With this pair of activities, students recreate the paragraph, first as a group, then independently. They end up with a paraphrased retelling of the paragraph that they can then use to support discussions or formative or summative writing they need to do as part of their Inquiry.

Joint Re-Writing from Notes to Create Paraphrased Summary

You will have read about Joint Construction in Chapter 4. The concept of joint construction is a pedagogically powerful one. Too often, students are treated to extensive modeling by the teacher and then expected to tackle a similar task by themselves. The gap between modeling and independent work can be too great for many students. Between the modeling phase and the independent work phase could be another phase where the teacher co-constructs with the students. This is to provide an opportunity for the students to "dance with an expert" – that is to actually be invited to produce a text but not to do it alone. Instead, to do it jointly with an expert writer to help out.

The first step is to create bulleted notes from the student texts with the underlining they did during the Detailed Reading. Here is what the student text would look like after the Detailed Reading:

> Student Copy of the Detailed Reading paragraph after the lesson. Shown with student underlining:
>
> 1. *Two things* happened <u>in the eighteenth century</u> that made it difficult for England to balance its trade with the East. 2. *First,* <u>the British</u> became <u>a nation of tea drinkers</u> and <u>the demand for Chinese tea rose astronomically</u>. 3. It is estimated that the average London worker spent five percent of his or her total household budget on tea. 4. *Second,* <u>northern Chinese</u>

Disciplinary Reading

> merchants began to ship Chinese cotton from the interior to the south to compete with the Indian cotton that Britain had used to help pay for its tea consumption habits. 5. To prevent a trade imbalance, the British tried to sell more of *their own products* to China, *but* there was not much demand for *heavy woolen fabrics* in a country accustomed to either cotton padding or silk.

You could have students take the lead in recording these for display. Notes from this text would be:

- in the eighteenth century
- the British
- a nation of tea drinkers
- the demand for Chinese tea rose astronomically
- northern Chinese merchants began to ship Chinese cotton
- to compete with the Indian cotton
- to prevent a trade imbalance
- the British
- tried to sell
- not much demand
- woolen fabrics

Incidentally, this stage provides the opportunity for students to work on the spelling. Invite students to take turns scribing on the board as other students read out the notes. Students can help the scribe spell the words. The next step is to write a text summary using the notes. Do this as a joint constructed activity, with either yourself or your students acting as the scribes. See Chapter 4, if needed, to remind yourself how to do Joint Construction.

Independent Re-Writing to Reconstruct the Paragraph

Guiding students to jointly construct a text from notes strongly prepares them for writing a successful text by themselves. However, the tasks involved in writing are very complex. They include knowing the topic, organizing the text, constructing appropriate sentences, choosing the right words, and spelling them correctly. So the more guided practice you give your students, the more successfully they will do all these tasks.

> ### If Students Need Additional Support with Independent Re-Writing
>
> Individual Construction is another step in guided practice before students have to write independently.
>
> - You erase the jointly constructed text from the board but leave the notes.
> - Students then have to write a new text using the notes.
>
> The task is to make their text as different as they can from the joint text. Some students will be able to do this without much help, which allows you to give more support to other students. Students can also start Individual Construction in groups.

As you'll no doubt realize, after the cycle of Detailed Reading, Joint Re-Writing, and Independent Re-Writing, students will have a deep understanding of the content of the text and the way the ideas are presented in chunks of meaning in the sentences. They will also have participated in a series of activities that integrated all components of the reading process: *Context and genre, Text and paragraph, Sentence and Word,* and *Word,* which is our way of addressing the problem identified in Factor 2: "Approaches to teaching reading that fragment the components of the reading process."

Summary

This chapter aimed to describe a supported approach to teaching disciplinary reading that makes visible how language serves the content at the text and genre level (Evoking the Story), the sentence and word group level (Detailed Reading), and the integration of all components of the reading process (Joint Re-Writing and Independent Re-Writing). At the same time, we focused on one high-leverage international move, the "prepare move" as a way of illustrating how we can have structured conversations about complex texts that make those texts accessible for all our learners. We hope you'll experiment and enjoy using these approaches. Furthermore, we hope that these approaches will help you support all your students in building towers.

Notes

1. pseudonym
2. Source unknown.
3. https://c3teachers.org/inquiries/imperialism/
4. https://c3teachers.org/inquiries/imperialism/
5. http://afe.easia.columbia.edu/

References

Fillmore, C. J. (1983). *Ideal readers and real readers*. Berkeley Cognitive Science Report No. 5.

Halliday, M.A.K., & Matthieessen, C. M.I.M. (2004). *An introduction to functional grammar*. Third Edition. Hodder Education.

Hopkins, J. (2017). *Language investigation packets one and two*. Course Materials developed for Edgewood College.

Ramírez, A. (2023). *Genre-based pedagogy and literacy instruction*. EBSCO Pathways to Research in Education.

Ramírez, A., Moyano, E. I., & Martin, J. R. (2021). A language-based theory of learning in the disciplines and for acting in social life. *Íkala, Revista de Lenguaje y Cultura*, 25(1), 11–15.

Rose, D., (2010). Reading to learn: accelerating learning and closing the gap. 2010 Edition. www.readingtolearn.com.au.

Rose, D. (2023). The Methodology of Reading to Learn. Downloaded on 7/28/23 from https://readingtolearn.com.au/pages/more-resources

Rose, D. & Martin, J. (2012) Learning to write, reading to learn: Genre, knowledge and pedagogy in the Sydney School. Equinox.

Westerlund, R., & Besser, S. (2021). Reconsidering Calkins' process writing pedagogy for multilingual learners: Units of Study in a fourth grade classroom (WCER Working Paper No. 2021-4). University of Wisconsin–Madison, Wisconsin Center for Education Research.

Wong Fillmore, L. (2009) Expectations and Diversity: Focus on English Learners and Their Instructional Needs. Expectations in Education. Readings on High Expectations, Effective Teaching and Student Achievement. Papers presented at the National Expectations Seminar. Las Vegas, Nevada. June 14–15, 2007.

Wong Fillmore, L., & Fillmore, C. (2013). What does text complexity mean for English learners and language minority students? *Understanding language* (pp. 1–11). Stanford University School of Education. http://www.icsi.berkeley.edu/pubs/ai/textcomplexity13.pdf

Chapter 5 Appendix (Tables 5.17–5.21)

Table 5.17 Full text from Table 5.8. Excerpt from Anchor Text: The Opium War and Foreign Encroachment

The Opium War and Foreign Encroachment[5]

Two things happened in the eighteenth century that made it difficult for England to balance its trade with the East. First, the British became a nation of tea drinkers and the demand for Chinese tea rose astronomically. It is estimated that the average London worker spent five percent of his or her total household budget on tea. Second, northern Chinese merchants began to ship Chinese cotton from the interior to the south to compete with the Indian cotton that Britain had used to help pay for its tea consumption habits. To prevent a trade imbalance, the British tried to sell more of their own products to China, but there was not much demand for heavy woolen fabrics in a country accustomed to either cotton padding or silk.

(*Continued*)

Disciplinary Reading

Table 5.17 (Continued)

The only solution was to increase the amount of Indian goods to pay for these Chinese luxuries, and increasingly in the seventeenth and eighteenth centuries, the item provided to China was Bengal opium. With greater opium supplies had naturally come an increase in demand and usage throughout the country, in spite of repeated prohibitions by the Chinese government and officials. The British did all they could to increase the trade: They bribed officials, helped the Chinese work out elaborate smuggling schemes to get the opium into China's interior, and distributed free samples of the drug to innocent victims.

The cost to China was enormous. The drug weakened a large percentage of the population (some estimate that 10 percent of the population regularly used opium by the late nineteenth century), and silver began to flow out of the country to pay for the opium. Many of the economic problems China faced later were either directly or indirectly traced to the opium trade. The government debated about whether to legalize the drug through a government monopoly like that on salt, hoping to barter Chinese goods in return for opium. But since the Chinese were fully aware of the harms of addiction, in 1838 the emperor decided to send one of his most able officials, Lin Tse-hsu (Lin Zexu, 1785–1850), to Canton (Guangzhou) to do whatever necessary to end the traffic forever.

Lin was able to put his first two proposals into effect easily. Addicts were rounded up, forcibly treated, and taken off the habit, and domestic drug dealers were harshly punished. His third objective – to confiscate foreign stores and force foreign merchants to sign pledges of good conduct, agreeing never to trade in opium and to be punished by Chinese law if ever found in violation – eventually brought war. Opinion in England was divided: Some British did indeed feel morally uneasy about the trade, but they were overruled by those who wanted to increase England's China trade and teach the arrogant Chinese a good lesson. Western military weapons, including percussion lock muskets, heavy artillery, and paddlewheel gunboats, were far superior to China's. Britain's troops had recently been toughened in the Napoleonic wars, and Britain could muster garrisons, warships, and provisions from its nearby colonies in Southeast Asia and India. The result was a disaster for the Chinese. By the summer of 1842, British ships were victorious and were even preparing to shell the old capital, Nanking (Nanjing), in central China. The emperor therefore had no choice but to accept the British demands and sign a peace agreement. This agreement, the first of the "unequal treaties," opened China to the West and marked the beginning of Western exploitation of the nation.

(Continued)

Table 5.17 (Continued)

Other humiliating defeats followed in what one historian has called China's "treaty century" (major aspects of the so-called "unequal treaties" were not formally voided until 1943). In 1843, France and the United States, and Russia in 1858, negotiated treaties similar to England's Nanking (Nanjing) Treaty, including a provision for extraterritoriality, whereby foreign nationals in China were immune from Chinese law. To compel a reluctant China to shift from its traditional tribute-based foreign relations to treaty relations, Europeans fought a second war with China from 1858–1860, and the concluding Treaty of Tientsin (Tianjin) and Convention of Peking (Beijing) increased China's semi-colonial status. More ports were open to foreign residence, trade, and foreigners, especially missionaries, were allowed free movement and business anywhere in the country.

Conflicts for the rest of the century wrung more humiliating concessions from China: With Russia over claims in China's far west and northeast in 1850 and 1860, with England over access to the upper reaches of the Yangtze River in 1876, with France over northern Vietnam in 1884, with Japan over its claims to Korea and northeast China in 1895, and with many foreign powers after 1897, which demanded "spheres of influence," especially for constructing railroads and mines. In 1900, an international army suppressed the anti-foreign Boxer Rebellion in northern China, destroying much of Beijing in the process. Each of these defeats brought more foreign demands, greater indemnities that China had to repay, more foreign presence along the coast, and more foreign participation in China's political and economic life. Little wonder that many in China were worried by the century's end that China was being sliced up "like a melon."

Table 5.18 Continued from Table 5.10 Evoking the Story Content Focus

Name the purpose for the students	Tell the students that the purpose of reading this text is to learn the content to answer the question, "How did the Opium Wars create foreign influence in China and how did China react?" Tell them they will use this content for the formative assessment assignment in which they write a paragraph answering that question.

(Continued)

Disciplinary Reading

Table 5.18 (Continued)

Overall text content summary	Summarize the text in a few sentences. You would say, for example: *This text is about imperialism and how that impacted China. It explains how the Opium Wars started and how foreigners got so involved in China.* Make connections to previous content learned as applicable: *Let's remind ourselves about trade imbalances and what that means, that concept is really important in this text. Remember the activity we did where we acted out trade imbalances. Some of you had pencils with no erasers that you were trying to trade for sticks of gum. How did that work out?*
Paragraph 1 Preview	Summarize the paragraph in a few sentences and leave room for the students to discover what happens through their own reading. You would say, for example: *This first paragraph tells us how the trade imbalance first began. The British people wanted Chinese tea, and they had to figure out something to trade with China to pay for the tea. Britain had a bunch of cotton from India so they used that. But something happens so Britain has to find something else to trade.* You could invite students to jot a few notes, or a key question on their text to help them focus their reading, for example: (note-taking) *Everyone take a minute and write, What happened that made it so Britain couldn't trade cotton anymore?*
Paragraph 2 Preview Students take notes	You would say: *The trade imbalance continued. Britain got sneaky. They decided to sell opium from their colony India.* [Have you already discussed opium and made connections to the opioid epidemic, if not do that here.] *Read this paragraph to figure out how opium solved Britain's trade imbalance problem.* (note-taking) *Everyone write, opium solves the trade imbalance in the margin of your text.*
Paragraph 3 Preview Students take notes	You would say something like this: *As you can imagine, Opium had very bad consequences for China. Many, many people got addicted, and the Chinese government decided to take action. This paragraph is going to tell you about the government's plans.* (Note-taking) *Let's write in the margin, opium epidemic! What is the government going to do?*

Table 5.18 (Continued)

Paragraph 4 Preview Students take notes	You would say something like this: *This paragraph is about this guy, named Lin Tse-hsu. The emperor of China appointed him to take care of the opium epidemic, by any means necessary. Let's just say not everyone was a fan of his tactics. Britain was particularly annoyed by these tactics and read to find out what it does to get revenge.* (Note-taking) *Lin. Britain reacts. What's going to happen?*
Paragraph 5 Preview Students take notes	You would say something like this: *Spoiler alert. What happens in paragraph 4 is we have the first Opium War. This one ended with a treaty, which the author calls an "unequal treaty"* [do students know what a treaty is? means? If not explain that here]. *It was a humiliating defeat for China and there were more humiliating defeats to come. The foreigners just kept coming. It was not pretty for China. Read to find out how China gets completely taken advantage of and turned into a colony.* (Note-taking) *wars, treaties, foreigners in China*
Paragraph 6 Preview Students take notes	You would say something like this: *This last paragraph tells us what happened the rest of the eighteenth century, how not just England, but other foreign powers came in and took control of various parts and businesses of China. This is when the Boxer Rebellion took place, which we will go into in a lot of detail next week. Read this to figure out why China felt like it was being sliced up like a melon and why the Boxer Rebellion took place.* (note-taking) *foreign powers in China, Boxer Rebellion*

Disciplinary Reading

Table 5.19 Continued from 5.12: Genre Structure Mapped with Text

	Paraphrased text	Original text	Genre Structure
1	It's the end of the eighteenth century. British people wanted Chinese tea, so Britain sold cotton they got from India to pay for the tea. But it turned out that China grew its own cotton, and didn't want it from Britain. So Britain had to find something else to sell. They tried wool, they had a lot of sheep making wool in Britain, but China didn't want British wool, they preferred silk and cotton for their clothes.	Two things happened in the eighteenth century that made it <u>difficult for England to balance its trade with the East</u>. First, the British became a nation of tea drinkers and the demand for Chinese tea rose astronomically. It is estimated that the average London worker spent five percent of his or her total household budget on tea. Second, northern Chinese merchants began to ship Chinese cotton from the interior to the south to compete with the Indian cotton that Britain had used to help pay for its tea consumption habits. To prevent a trade imbalance, the British tried to sell more of their own products to China, but there was not much demand for heavy woolen fabrics in a country accustomed to either cotton padding or silk.	<u>Factor 1</u> Trade Imbalance that started with a problem and attempts to solve the problem **Problem:** Britain wanted Chinese tea, but didn't have anything to trade for it that China wanted **Solution:** Britain tries cotton, then wool **Reactions:** China rejects cotton, wool

(*Continued*)

Table 5.19 (Continued)

	Paraphrased text	Original text	Genre Structure
2	Britain needed another thing to sell. They decided to sell opium from Bengal (India). There was a lot of demand for opium, so this solved Britain's trade imbalance, they traded opium and got all the tea they needed. But this caused another problem. The Chinese government did not want the opium because it was not healthy for its people. Chinese officials tried to ban use of opium. But the British kept selling opium.	The only solution was to increase the amount of Indian goods to pay for these Chinese luxuries, and increasingly in the seventeenth and eighteenth centuries the item provided to China was Bengal opium. With greater opium supplies had naturally come an increase in demand and usage throughout the country, in spite of repeated prohibitions by the Chinese government and officials. The British did all they could to increase the trade: They bribed officials, helped the Chinese work out elaborate smuggling schemes to get the opium into China's interior, and distributed free samples of the drug to innocent victims.	**Factor 1** **(continued)** **Problem from Paragraph 1 (continued)** Britain wanted Chinese tea, but didn't have anything to trade for it that China wanted **Solution:** Britain tries opium **Reactions:** China accepts opium on the Black Market, but the demand and sale continues.

(*Continued*)

Disciplinary Reading

Table 5.19 (Continued)

	Paraphrased text	Original text	Genre Structure
3	Opium had very bad consequences for China. Chinese people got addicted (10 percent of all people were affected). Chinese people started paying for opium with silver (another trade imbalance because now China was spending more than it was bringing in from the price Britain was paying for tea). To try and solve the opium problem, the Chinese emperor assigned Official Lin to do whatever means necessary.	The cost to China was enormous. The drug weakened a large percentage of the population (some estimate that 10 percent of the population regularly used opium by the late nineteenth century), and silver began to flow out of the country to pay for the opium. Many of the economic problems China faced later were either directly or indirectly traced to the opium trade. The government debated about whether to legalize the drug through a government monopoly like that on salt, hoping to barter Chinese goods in return for opium. But since the Chinese were fully aware of the harms of addiction, in 1838 the emperor decided to send one of his most able officials, Lin Tse-hsu (Lin Zexu, 1785–1850), to Canton (Guangzhou) to do whatever necessary to end the traffic forever.	Factor 2 **Problem**: Chinese people buy opium from the British. Large numbers get addicted. **Solution**: Chinese government tries to stop the epidemic by cracking down on the sale of opium, but sales continue.

Table 5.19 (Continued)

	Paraphrased text	Original text	Genre Structure
4	What did Lin do? 1. Rounded up addicts and got them off opium 2. Punished domestic opium dealers 3. Confiscated foreign supplies of opium, and forced foreign merchants to agree not to sell opium to China or they would be punished by Chinese law #3 resulted in the first Opium War. What did Britain think about Lin's efforts? People had different opinions: Some felt guilty about the bad things that were happening to Chinese people because of the opium addiction. Others wanted to sell more and more things to China and were annoyed that Lin was trying to stop them from doing this (this opinion won). Britain went to war with China. Britain had lots of weapons, ships, and supplies from its colonies in Southeast Asia and India. British ships attacked China from the coast and threatened to bomb the old capital Nanjing. This made the emperor surrender and sign a peace agreement with Britain. This agreement made it so that Britain and other countries from the west could sell things to China. The author calls this the first of the "unequal treaties." Claim – this treaty marked the beginning of the Western exploitation of China.	Lin was able to put his first two proposals into effect easily. Addicts were rounded up, forcibly treated, and taken off the habit, and domestic drug dealers were harshly punished. His third objective – to confiscate foreign stores and force foreign merchants to sign pledges of good conduct, agreeing never to trade in opium and to be punished by Chinese law if ever found in violation – eventually brought war. Opinion in England was divided: Some British did indeed feel morally uneasy about the trade, but they were overruled by those who wanted to increase England's China-trade and teach the arrogant Chinese a good lesson. Western military weapons, including percussion lock muskets, heavy artillery, and paddlewheel gunboats, were far superior to China's. Britain's troops had recently been toughened in the Napoleonic wars, and Britain could muster garrisons, warships, and provisions from its nearby colonies in Southeast Asia and India. The result was a disaster for the Chinese. By the summer of 1842, British ships were victorious and were even preparing to shell the old capital, Nanking (Nanjing), in central China. The emperor therefore had no choice but to accept the British demands and sign a peace agreement. <u>This agreement, the first of the "unequal treaties," opened China to the West and marked the beginning of Western exploitation of the nation.</u>	**Reactions:** China Confiscates foreign supplies of opium, and forces foreign merchants to agree not to sell opium to China or they would be punished by Chinese law. **Reactions:** Britain. Public opinion mixed. War. **Factor 3:** Chinese defeat in the Opium War provides an opening for foreigners to come in and do business and missionary work.

(Continued)

Disciplinary Reading

Table 5.19 (Continued)

	Paraphrased text	Original text	Genre Structure
5	What happened next? More foreign encroachment: More unequal treaties for China. France and the United States, and Russia made treaties like the first one Britain made, "unequal treaties." As part of this treaty, they put in a rule that foreigners didn't have to follow Chinese law. Chinese did not want this, so the Europeans fought another war with China and won. The result of this second war was that foreigners could live in China and sell what they wanted. Missionaries could come too. All the foreigners could go wherever they wanted in the country and do what they wanted.	Other humiliating defeats followed in what one historian has called China's "treaty century" (major aspects of the so-called "unequal treaties" were not formally voided until 1943). In 1843, France and the United States, and Russia in 1858, negotiated treaties similar to England's Nanking (Nanjing) Treaty, including a provision for extraterritoriality, whereby foreign nationals in China were immune from Chinese law. To compel a reluctant China to shift from its traditional tribute-based foreign relations to treaty relations, Europeans fought a second war with China from 1858–1860, and the concluding Treaty of Tientsin (Tianjin) and Convention of Peking (Beijing) increased China's semi-colonial status. More ports were open to foreign residence, trade, and foreigners, especially missionaries, were allowed free movement and business anywhere in the country.	**Factor 3:** Chinese defeat in the Opium War provides an opening for foreigners to come in and do business and missionary work. **Problem (continued from Paragraph 4):** China is defeated. There are a series of "unequal treaties" that disadvantage China. **Solution (continued from Paragraph 4):** China fights back, and there is another war, China loses again. **Reactions:** Foreigners (and not just British) keep encroaching and colonizing China.

(Continued)

Table 5.19 (Continued)

	Paraphrased text	Original text	Genre Structure
6	What happened next? Even more foreign encroachment: Rest of eighteenth century, China was forced to give up more things: Russia got land – far west and northeast. England got access to the Yangtze River. France got Northern Vietnam. Japan got Korea and northeast China. Other foreign powers got control to build railroads and mines. Chinese fought back in 1900, this was the Boxer Rebellion, but lost to an international army and much of Beijing was destroyed. Each defeat brought more foreign demands, More debts China had to pay, More foreign presence on the coast, More foreign participation in China's political and economic life.	Conflicts for the rest of the century wrung more humiliating concessions from China: With Russia over claims in China's far west and northeast in 1850 and 1860, with England over access to the upper reaches of the Yangtze River in 1876, with France over northern Vietnam in 1884, with Japan over its claims to Korea and northeast China in 1895, and with many foreign powers after 1897 which demanded "spheres of influence," especially for constructing railroads and mines. In 1900, an international army suppressed the anti-foreign Boxer Rebellion in northern China, destroying much of Beijing in the process. Each of these defeats brought more foreign demands, greater indemnities that China had to repay, <u>more foreign presence along the coast, and more foreign participation in China's political and economic life.</u> Little wonder that many in China were worried by the century's end that <u>China was being sliced up "like a melon."</u>	**Factor 3** (continued from Paragraph 4) **Problem** (continued from Paragraph 4): China is defeated. There are a series of "unequal treaties" that disadvantage China. **Solution:** China fights back, and there is another war, China loses again, and then rebels with the Boxer Rebellion. **Reactions:** Foreigners (and not just British) keep encroaching and colonizing China. **Outcome:** China becomes politically weak, and colonized by western nations (Britain, Russia, France).

Disciplinary Reading

Table 5.20 Analysis of Elements of Meaning, Participants, Processes, Circumstances

---

1. <u>Two things</u> happened in the eighteenth century [that made it difficult for England to balance its trade with the East]. 2. First, <u>the British</u> became <u>a nation of tea drinkers and</u> [the demand for Chinese tea rose astronomically]. 3. <u>It</u> is estimated [that the average London worker spent five percent of his or her total household budget on tea]. 4. Second, <u>northern Chinese merchants</u> began to ship <u>Chinese cotton</u> from the interior to the south to compete with the Indian cotton [that Britain had used to help pay for its tea consumption habits]. 5. To prevent <u>a trade imbalance</u>, <u>the British</u> tried to sell [more of their own products to China], but <u>there</u> was [not much demand for heavy woolen fabrics in a country accustomed to either cotton padding or silk].

Table 5.21 Continued from Table 5.15 Detailed Reading Script for Paragraph 1 of *The Opium War and Foreign Encroachment*

What the teacher is doing	What the teacher would say
Orientation to the social purpose	1. Imagine all the students have this text in front of them. You've told the students what the social purpose of the text is – *That this is a factorial explanation whose job it is to explain how the trade imbalance between Britain and China came about.*
Paragraph Summary (Prepare)	2. Then, you tell them you are going to have them look at the first paragraph. You tell them something like, *In this paragraph we're going to hear about how the trade imbalance started. British people wanted Chinese tea, so Britain sold Indian cotton to China to pay for the tea. This was balanced, but then China didn't want the cotton Britain was trading for the tea. So Britain had to find something else to sell. They tried wool fabrics, but China didn't want what Britain had to sell (heavy woolen fabrics). So the imbalance was that Britain wanted what China had, but China didn't want anything Britain had to trade.*
Sentence Summary (Prepare)	3. You say something like, *The first sentence is a preview that tells us that there are two things that made it difficult for England to balance trade with China.*
Read aloud	4. You read: *Two things happened in the eighteenth century that made it difficult for England to balance its trade with the East.*

(Continued)

Table 5.21 (Continued)

What the teacher is doing	What the teacher would say
Prepare Focus Students underline Sentence Summary (Prepare) Read aloud	5. (Prep) *This sentence tells us when this trade imbalance began.* (Focus) *When did this begin, Marcus?* [in the eighteenth century]. *That's right, let's underline that.* 6. You say something like *the second sentence tells us about the first factor, which is that all of a sudden, most people in Britain started drinking tea, which came from China, and wanted lots and lots of Chinese tea.* 7. You read: *First, the British became a nation of tea drinkers and the demand for Chinese tea rose astronomically.*
Focus Students underline Prepare Focus Focus Students underline Elaborate? Prepare Focus	8. (Focus) *Who is this sentence about? Allyson?* [the British] *that's right, let's underline that.* 9. *The first part of this sentence tells us that the British hadn't always drunk a lot of tea, but that what happened was a change.* (Focus) *What word tells us that what happened was a change? Lucy?* [became]. *That's right.* 10. (Focus) *The British became what? James?* [a nation of tea drinkers]. *Excellent, go ahead and underline a nation of tea drinkers.* (Do they know about the British culture of drinking tea that still exists today? Maybe elaborate upon this.)
Elaborate Students underline	11. (Prep) *The second part of this sentence tells us that because the British people now wanted to drink a lot of tea, the demand for Chinese tea increased.* (Focus) *What word tells us that the demand rose a lot? Chenita?* [astronomically]. *Right.* (Elaborate) *astronomically means it rose a lot and it rose quickly. Let's underline this whole clause, "the demand rose astronomically."*
Sentence Summary (Prepare) Read aloud Prepare Focus Focus	12. You say something like *sentence number 3 really just elaborates what was said in sentence 2. It tells us more about how much tea the British people were drinking at that time and how important it was to them.* (Do they need reminding that London is the capital of Britain?)

(Continued)

Disciplinary Reading

Table 5.21 (Continued)

What the teacher is doing	What the teacher would say
	13. You read: *It is estimated that the average London worker spent five percent of his or her total household budget on tea.*
	14. (Prep) *The sentence begins with the word, it, but it is not used in the usual way, instead it means something like everyone, people that have studied this topic, books on this topic* (Focus) *Who is "it" referring to in this sentence? Susanna?* [people, historians].
	15. *Right* (Focus) *And what did those people and historians estimate? Mike?* (that the average London spent five percent of his or her household budget on tea). (Could elaborate here on the significance or push that discussion to later.)
Read aloud Prepare Students annotate Sentence Summary (Prepare) Focus Students Underline Prepare Focus Prepare Focus Students underline Focus	16. You read the next sentence: *Second, northern Chinese merchants began to ship Chinese cotton from the interior to the south to compete with the Indian cotton that Britain had used to help pay for its tea consumption habits.*
	17. (Prepare) *Second. When texts have a second, there is always a first. What was the first thing that happened that started the trade imbalance? Clara?* (The British starting drinking lots of tea.) *What was the first thing? Everyone circle two things in sentence 1 and then draw arrows to First and Second.*
	18. You say something like: *There is a lot going on in this sentence. It's telling us about how China reacted to Britain trying to trade cotton from India for the tea. China didn't need the cotton because they had their own cotton; it was just in the north of the country.*
	19. (Focus) *Let's look at this more closely, who began to ship the Chinese cotton? Mark?* (northern Chinese merchants). *Yes. Let's underline that whole phrase, from northern Chinese merchants to Chinese cotton.*
	20. (Prepare) *This sentence then tells us where they shipped the cotton from.* (Focus) *Where was this? Amy?* (From the interior to the south.)
	21. *Right,* (Prepare) *next it tells us why the Chinese started shipping this cotton.* (Focus) *Why did they do this? Jose?* (To compete with the Indian cotton.) *Good. Let's underline to compete with the Indian cotton.*
	22. (Focus) *Ok, now what else does this sentence tell us about the Indian cotton? John?* (That Britain had used it to help pay for its tea consumption habits.)

(Continued)

Disciplinary Reading

Table 5.21 (Continued)

What the teacher is doing	What the teacher would say
Sentence Summary (Prepare) Read aloud	23. You summarize the last sentence something like this: *This sentence tells us how the British tried to prevent a trade imbalance and reacted to China selling their own cotton and competing with the cotton they were selling. What Britain did was to try and sell other things they had, like wool fabrics. But the Chinese didn't need or want the wool, so the trade balance continued.*
	24. You read: *To prevent a trade imbalance, the British tried to sell more of their own products to China, but there was not much demand for heavy woolen fabrics in a country accustomed to either cotton padding or silk.*
Prepare Focus Students underline Focus Students underline Prepare Focus Students underline Elaborate Focus Students annotate Focus Students annotate Focus Students underline Prepare Focus Elaborate Students Underline	25. (Prep) *This sentence starts by telling us what's happening.* (Focus) *What are the words that tell us what happened? Darius?* (to prevent). *That's right, go ahead and underline to prevent.*
	26. (Focus) *To prevent what? Savannah?* (A trade imbalance.) *Good. Let's underline that.*
	27. (Prep) *Next it tells us who tried to prevent the trade imbalance.* (Focus) *Who was that? Joseph?* (the British). *Right. Let's underline the British* (Elaborate). *Because the Chinese didn't want the Indian cotton the British were trying to trade for all the tea they wanted, so they decided to sell their own products.* (Focus) *It gives us an example of their own products. What is an example of this? Ginger?* (Heavy woolen fabrics.) *OK, let's draw an arrow from their own products to heavy woolen fabrics.*
	28. (Focus) *There is a really important word here that tells us that this didn't work, that the British were not able to sell their woolen fabrics to the Chinese. Oscar?* (but). *Right, let's circle that.*
	29. (Focus) *But what? Juliette?* (There was not much demand for the heavy woolen fabrics.) *Good, let's underline not much demand.*
	30. *That's right,* (Prepare) *the last part of the sentence tells us why.* (Focus) *Why? Thomas?* (It says they were accustomed to either cotton padding or silk.) *You are right,* (Elab) *what that means is the Chinese still needed warm clothes, but instead of wool, they had other fabric to keep them warm and those fabrics were cotton and silk, silk with cotton underneath it is really warm. Ok, let's underline tried to sell, then woolen fabrics. Then let's annotate this by writing, "but the Chinese didn't want them."*

Disciplinary Reading

Chapter 5 Answer Key

Table 5.4 Student-Led Discussion

	Speaker	Dialogue	What's going on?
1	Teacher	OK, you are going to discuss this text in your small groups. Focus on Yü Hsien, what he did and why you think he was important.	Explains the task. Sets a focus prompt.
2	Calvin	He was the one behind the Boxers; he had permission from the Empress to promote all the killing of the foreigners.	Initiates the discussion by responding to the teacher's focus prompt.
3	Destiny	He gave people a reward.	Adds on to Calvin's response.
4	Jada	Really? That's so messed up.	Responds to Calvin and Destiny's contributions. Demonstrates understanding of Calvin and Destiny's responses, but does not add further content. Did she read the text?
5	Destiny	I know, right.	Affirms Jada's response.
6	Calvin	We should talk about why he was important. What do you guys think?	Re-focuses the group. Invites a response.
7	Caleb and Jada	[no response, blank looks, seems like they didn't read the text]	No response.
8	Destiny	Well, I think he was important because he was so powerful, I mean he got an entire group of people to hate the foreigners and to want to kill them.	Responds, builds on Calvin's response in Line 2 and makes inferential meaning of the text.
9	Calvin	Yeah, it's amazing they listened to him.	Affirms Destiny's response.
10	Teacher	Ok, let's all come back and share.	Reconvenes the class back into a whole group.

5.15 In 1900, an international army suppressed the anti-foreign Boxer Rebellion in northern China.

When?	What?	What's happening?	What?	Where?
In 1900	an international army	suppressed	the anti-foreign Boxer Rebellion	in northern China.
Circumstance	Participant	Process	Participant	Circumstance

5.16 More ports were open to foreign residence and trade, and

What?	What's happening	What	Conjunction
More ports	Were open to	Foreign residence and trade	And
Participant	Process	Participant	Conjunction

foreigners, especially missionaries, were allowed free movement and business anywhere in the country.

Who	What kind	What's happening	What	Where
Foreigners	especially missionaries	were allowed	free movement and business	anywhere in the country
Participant	Circumstance	Process	Participant	Circumstance

5.17 Sentence 1: Two things happened in the eighteenth century [that made it difficult for England to balance its trade with the East].

What?	What's happening?	When?	What else?
Two things	happened	In the eighteenth century	that made it difficult for England to balance its trade with the East.
Participant	Process	Circumstance	Participant

207

Disciplinary Reading

5.18 Sentence 2: First, the British became a nation of tea drinkers and the demand for Chinese tea rose astronomically.

Text connective	What	What's happening	What?	
First	The British	became	a nation of tea drinkers	
Text connective	*Participant*	*Process*	*Participant*	
Conjunction	What?	**What kind?**	What's happening	**how?**
And	the demand	for Chinese tea	rose	astronomically
Conjunction	*Process*	*circumstance*	*Process*	*circumstance*

5.19 Sentence 3: It is estimated that the average London worker spent five percent of his or her total household budget on tea.

What?	What's happening	conjunction	Who	What's happening	What	How?
It	is estimated	that	the average London worker	spent	five percent of his or her total budget	on tea
Participant	*Process*	*Conjunction*	*Participant*	*Process*	*Participant*	*Circumstance*

Disciplinary Reading

5.20 Sentence 4: Second, northern Chinese merchants began to ship Chinese cotton from the interior to the south to compete with the Indian cotton [that Britain had used to help pay for its tea consumption habits].

Text Connective	What		What's happening	What?
Second	Northern Chinese merchants		Began to ship	Chinese cotton
Text Connective	Participant		Process	Participant
Where	**What's happening?**		**How?**	What else?
From the interior to the south	to compete		with the Indian cotton	that Britain has used to help pay for its tea consumption habits
Circumstance	Process		Circumstance	Participant

5.21 Sentence 5: To prevent a trade imbalance, the British tried to sell [more of their own products to China], but there was [not much demand for heavy woolen fabrics in a country accustomed to either cotton padding or silk].

What's happening	What?	Who	What's happening?	what?
To prevent	a trade balance	the British	tried to sell	More of their own products to China
Process Conjunction	Participant what?	Participant How are things related or defined?	Process what?	Participant
But	There	was		not much demand for heavy woolen fabrics in a country accustomed to either cotton padding or silk
Conjunction	Participant	Process		Participant

For Product Safety Concerns and Information please contact our EU representative GPSR@taylorandfrancis.com
Taylor & Francis Verlag GmbH, Kaufingerstraße 24, 80331 München, Germany

www.ingramcontent.com/pod-product-compliance
Lightning Source LLC
Chambersburg PA
CBHW050633300426
44112CB00012B/1780